GOURMET PRESERVES

Gourmet Preserves

JUDITH CHOATE

ILLUSTRATED BY MARTHA VAUGHAN

WEIDENFELD & NICOLSON

NEW YORK

Published by Weidenfeld & Nicolson, New York
A Division of Wheatland Corporation
10 East 53rd Street
New York, NY 10022

LIBRARY OF CONGRESS CATALOGING-IN-PUBLICATION DATA
Choate, Judith.
      Gourmet preserves
      Includes index.
      1. Canning and preserving.   I. Title.
TX601.C53   1987   641.4   86-18951
ISBN 1-55584-038-8

Manufactured in the United States of America by
The Maple Vail Book Mfg. Group, Inc.

Designed by Laurel Vaughan

First Edition

10 9 8 7 6 5 4 3 2 1

*To Jane—for kitchen
memories past and those yet
to come*

Contents

GOURMET PRESERVES

Introduction

Imported or domestic, locally produced or regionally manufactured, jellies, jams, and all measure of condiments and sauces are available to the American pantry. Gourmet shops, supermarkets, greengrocers, specialty shops, and mail-order catalogs abound with fine, exotic canned goods. But no matter how superb or unusual the commercial product, it will never equal the ultimate preserves made in your own kitchen.

This book is for the experienced cook who wants to produce small amounts of the very best preserves. Sweet or savory, spread, sauce, or condiment, these are recipes to give your own menus that extra gusto and provide the perfect on-hand gift for fellow food lovers.

The surge of interest in foods American, the proliferation of "American restaurants" featuring "nouvelle American" cuisine, and the Americanization of international recipes have led us back to the discovery of our native cuisine. Our forefathers ate and preserved far more foods than most 20th-century Americans will ever taste. Many foods that we now consider gourmet or special were frequently on the average person's plate in the last century: game, wild greens, "free range" chicken, unadulterated meats, native herbs and fruits. Items for which we will now pay extra were once just plain food. It is interesting to note that gourmet preserving is not new, just rediscovered.

The history of "putting foods by" has been greatly enhanced by American ingenuity. From the early colonists' preservation of new and different native foodstuffs for times of scarcity to the freeze-dried meals of the 20th century, Americans have constantly created inventive ways to store foods. However, it was the advent of the 19th-century Shaker communities that most profoundly affected American preserving.

The Shakers' arrival in America, in 1774, heralded the beginning of a new life for the colonies. It was a time of change and freedom, a time for new thought and creation. As the Revolution freed the colonies from England, the colonists strove to establish a truly American life. Bringing traditional preserving methods with them from the Old Country, colonists began to expand their preserving skills using natural American foodstuffs. Even Martha Washington, as First Lady, became an advocate of American cooking, and a time for culinary invention began.

By the mid-1860s the Shaker community had grown from seven members to several communities with thousands of members in many states. Each community not only was self-sufficient but grew and made enough to sell to the outside world. Shaker kitchens were models of efficiency and cleanliness and were the earliest example of mass production. The canning kitchens were equipped (and still are, in both museum and contemporary living settlements) with huge stoves, great copper canning kettles, and pristine spaces in cupboards and on long trestle tables to facilitate the mass production of preserved foods. Filled with conveniences and inventions far more advanced than those of the general population, the Shaker canning kitchen created a wide demand for products carrying the Shaker label. The quality, integrity, and care that characterized these products established, for the American housewife, a high standard to duplicate in her own kitchen.

In fact, in areas where Shaker communities flourished it was not at all unusual for an outside family to take its own produce to be preserved by the Shaker sisters. Their recipes used the best they could grow, were seasoned with imagination, and were stored in the most beautifully crafted containers they could create. Not only did they cook, they did so with inventiveness, skill, and with the knowledge that food was one of God's rewards. This is the heritage that is the basis for the current interest in our native cuisine, of which preserving and freezing the best foodstuffs one can is an integral part.

The wide availability of a variety of fresh fruits, vegetables, and herbs has now made it possible to prepare canned goods all year long. However, it is always preferable to use local products during their individual growing seasons. January's picture-perfect *hard* tomato, the *stored* apple of March, and the year-round *frozen* strawberry all have a fraction of the taste, smell, and texture of their garden-fresh counterparts. When you can, do your preserving seasonally. When this is not possible, purchase the best available to you (from either a supermarket, a greengrocer, or a local wholesaler). You can also experiment with the exotic produce now imported from around the world for American consumption. The end result will be well worth the extra time, effort, and money you put into selecting quality ingredients for your gourmet preserves.

What are gourmet preserves? Unique combinations, careful flavoring, color, and pure, clean taste are the most important components of what should be a welcome addition to any menu and should turn a mundane meal into an extraordinary dining experience. No grape jelly or dill pickles here!

Gourmet preserves evolved from our American culinary heritage. They combine the best of the old with the convenience and availability of the new. It is the legacy of our forefathers (and -mothers), the integrity and ingenuity of the Shakers, and the cook's flare for experimentation and discriminating taste that combine to produce gourmet preserves. Every wonderful food that we know as American can be brought to the table from a bag, a carton, a jar, a can, or a crock. Just let this book be your guide.

1

General Information

- Always plan in advance. Preserving is not a "spur of the moment" inspiration.
- Familiarize yourself with the processes you will be using. Like general cooking, preserving is much easier when you don't have to remember the basics while involved in the step-by-step routine.
- Your equipment must be clean, free of cracks, chips, or rust. Spoilage is frequently caused by the use of unclean or damaged equipment.
- Keep your work area uncluttered and free of unnecessary utensils or jars.
- Use the exact ingredients as directed in each recipe.
- Make sure you have sufficient containers with lids that fit. (I generally sterilize a couple of extra jars and lids, just in case I end up with more to can than the recipe states.)
- Prepare only the exact amount of fruit or vegetables required. Everything in each batch should be of the same ripeness and quality.

• Measure out the ingredients before you begin. This will ensure against the loss of a batch of preserves when an essential ingredient is, at the last and most inopportune moment, missing.

• If you will be using the steam pressure or water bath method, be certain you are familiar with their individual cooking processes.

• Keep all jars and lids in their hot sterilizing baths until ready for use. Remove one jar at a time.

• All canning jars must be hot when being filled with hot foods or liquids.

• Fill and seal one container at a time.

• No matter what processing method is used, all lids, rims, and edges must be clean and free of food before sealing.

• Always cool filled jars before placing in the freezer or on a very cold surface.

• Label everything you preserve with its name, date, and shelf life.

• And, above all, don't rush! There are *no safe shortcuts* to be taken when making gourmet preserves.

HOW TO SELECT AND PREPARE FOODS FOR PRESERVING

Looking through my grandmother's canning notes, I found this cardinal rule: "One hour from garden to can." This is generally impossible today and, with modern refrigeration and storage, no longer really necessary. However, *fresh is best!*

All fruits and vegetables should be firm, free of blemishes, and as fresh as possible. Fruits should be well ripened and vegetables crisp. Unless otherwise specified, all ingredients in a given recipe should be of consistent quality and ripeness.

If you garden, or have a farmer's market or orchard nearby, you can be assured of freshness. If you must rely on your supermarket produce manager or neighborhood greengrocer, make friends, give bribes, and pay extra to get the best obtainable. It is smart, both for economy and taste, to do as much preserving as you can during your area's growing season. The finished product is only enhanced by the perfection of the ingredients.

As new and unusual produce (and other food products) are imported from around the world, try to incorporate them into your preserving. I am constantly amazed at the availability of fresh herbs, tropical produce, and exotic vegetables, and I have experimented with all of them. If you see an untried fruit or vegetable, buy a small amount for tasting and comparing. Once you have identified its properties, adapt it to your usual recipes. For instance, all berries are just about interchangeable. And kiwi can be used in place of any soft, juicy fruit. Don't be afraid to experiment. If you do so in small batches, you can generally enjoy a new taste treat or salvage what could have been a disaster.

All of the products used in preserving—seasonings, herbs, dried fruits or vegetables, chocolate, and so forth—should be of the highest quality. Imported or most expensive is not necessarily the best, so do some research before buying. Each recipe will give a recommended type or style, but you might also want to experiment with what is available to you.

Clean all ingredients thoroughly. Leafy vegetables, berries, and herbs should be inspected for sand or grit. A spray wash will assist in removing it. Root vegetables should be scrubbed.

Dry thoroughly. Fragile foods such as berries should be drained dry on towels or newspaper.

Peaches, nectarines, apricots, and tomatoes are easily peeled by immersing, for about 30 seconds, in a pot of boiling water to loosen the skin. Remove from boiling water and dip into cold water. The skin will slip off ripe fruit and, with a bit of assistance with a paring knife, off not-so-ripe fruit.

Berries are stemmed and are usually left whole. All other fruits and vegetables should be stemmed, peeled or skinned, seeded, and cut as directed.

If a recipe calls for cooked fruits or vegetables, add the least amount of water you can to prevent sticking. I generally add no water for soft fruits and vegetables and no more than one cup per quart of raw, hard fruits or vegetables. Cover and simmer over very low heat until the fruit or vegetable is just cooked through. Do not overcook if it is being used in a recipe that requires further cooking.

All other ingredients should be fresh and measured out before proceeding with the recipe. This will make the processing much simpler as well as ensure that you have everything you need on hand before continuing with the final preparation.

EQUIPMENT

Most equipment required for gourmet preserving will be found on your kitchen shelves, as you will need nothing out of the ordinary. Since we are dealing with quality rather than quantity, you will not even need the huge kettles required for the basic canning of the past.

More than any other modern convenience, the food processor has eliminated much of the drudgery of kitchen chores. As an aid in preserving, it grinds, chops, blends, and peels with the least waste and mess. As a time saver, it is even better!

All of your equipment must be very clean and free of rust, chips, or scratches.

TO EASE YOUR JOB YOU WILL WANT TO HAVE ON HAND:

• Food processor (a blender, food grinder, or food mill can also be used)
• Heavy kettle for cooking jams, jellies, relishes, et cetera
• Large pot (with lid) for use as a boiling water bath
• Measuring cups and spoons
• Wooden spoons
• Large metal spoon
• Funnel
• Ladle with pouring spout
• Spatula
• Jar lifter or tongs
• Strainer (a colander with cheesecloth or a sieve can also be used)
• Clean cloths for wiping jars
• Paraffin with disposable container for melting

Extras (not necessary but nice to have):

- Kitchen scale
- Wire racks for cooling
- Jelly bag
- Prepared labels
- Water bath canner or steam pressure canner

Canning Jars

It is not essential to purchase standard home canning jars, but if you want to have a uniform look and make a special presentation, it is worth doing. You can, in most areas, purchase them at grocery, hardware, or variety stores. Fancy canning jars are frequently featured in gourmet food and cookware mail-order catalogs. If you have any difficulty locating standard canning jars, contact: Consumer Service Department, Ball Brothers Company, Muncie, Ind. 47302 (317-747-6257).

There are two types of jars easily obtainable for today's home canning:

• The can or freeze jar, which, as its name implies, can be used for either home canning or freezing. This jar will require the standard two-part metal cover, which consists of a flat rubber-edged sealing lid and a screw cap.

• The lightening jar, either domestic or imported, is used only for canning. It has a glass domelike lid that seals with a rubber ring. The lid is held tight by a wire clamp.

If you want to reuse jars you have saved (from commercially canned products) for home canning, be sure that they are free of nicks and have smooth inner surfaces, and that the tops and caps form a perfect fit. If possible use jars that will take the standard home-canning two-part cover. If not, you will have to seal them with melted paraffin. To melt paraffin you need a small disposable container (a one-pound coffee can or old coffee pot with spout is good) and a heat-proof pan in which to place the container while melting paraffin over direct heat.

Whatever jar you use, it must be freshly sterilized and free of soap or odors. All rubber sealing lids or rings should be unused and sterile.

Canners

If you decide you are going to do extensive home canning, you may want to purchase a steam pressure canner and/or a water bath canner. Both of these are available through Sears Roebuck and Co.

A steam pressure canner is a very large pressure cooker (about 22 quarts) with a tight-fitting lid and a steam valve. This kettle is used to process foods under pressure at high temperatures. It is the only home method that will destroy the bacteria that causes botulism and other severe types of spoilage in low-acid foods.

A water bath canner is a deep kettle with a wire basket insert that holds about eight jars. The kettle will hold enough water to cover the jars without boiling over. It is used to preserve foods high in acids that do not require the high pressure of a steam pressure canner.

Both of these canners require special attention to the manufacturer's instructions. Neither are difficult or dangerous, but the steam pressure canner in particular needs watching and a thorough understanding of its use.

METHODS OF PRESERVING

Preserving is, quite simply, a method of holding foods, sealed and free of contamination, for future eating and is, as such, an ancient ritual. I would guess that as soon as man discovered food he discovered a way to "put it by."

To prevent starvation, early man is presumed to have first dried those foods available to him in times of plenty. Fire and salt expanded his preserving repertoire, and freezing was improvised as a measure to keep foods longer. Until the 1800s these were the only methods available.

Canning, the results of which line our supermarket shelves, was an early 19th-century American invention. First used in the 1820s, tin cans did not come into widespread use until 1885, when a machine that stamped them out was patented. This offered a surefire method of preserving all manner of foodstuffs and took canning out of the home and into commerce.

Refrigeration greatly increased the life of all foods, both in the home and in the marketplace. The advent of the iceman brought the storage of perishable goods into the kitchen and gave birth to a new appliance. The root cellar and cold storage were replaced with the icebox. Mechanical refrigeration further revolutionized food storage and greatly expanded year-round availability of produce from around the world. By the end of World War II, almost every kitchen had an electric refrigerator that offered some freezing capacity.

Quick freezing is, of course, the latest technique for the home preservation of food. It is less time-consuming than the other, older methods and generally the one that most nearly reproduces the original.

No matter which method is used, there is no easy way to produce gourmet preserves. Recipes must be followed, each method learned. If you don't have time to do it, don't start. (The only exception to this rule is: You may prepare the raw produce and have all ingredients ready up to 24 hours prior to actual processing.)

All of the early methods remain today, many with little change. To preserve foods you may dehydrate, smoke, salt, cool, freeze, or can. With gourmet preserves, however, we will deal only with the canning, freezing, or refrigeration of fruits, vegetables (in many guises), and sauces. Each recipe will give a recommended method that must be followed. Again, *do not take shortcuts!*

Preserving Methods

1. OPEN KETTLE. This is used for jams, jellies, conserves, marmalades, butters, spiced fruit, chutneys, most cooked sauces, some cooked relishes, condiments, and pickles. It requires that the food be cooked to boiling, in either a sugar or a vinegar base, and immediately poured into hot sterilized jars that are sealed with sterilized rubber-edged lids and screw caps. Food prepared by the open-kettle method have, approximately, a one-year shelf life.

General directions for open-kettle canning: Cook foods for the specified length of time in a large uncovered pot. Pour when boiling hot into hot sterilized jars, one jar at a time. Wipe sealing edges with clean, dry cloth. Seal, one jar at a time, with hot sterilized lids and caps. Turn jar over quickly to heat lid. Turn upright.

Place jars about two inches apart on wire racks or newspaper, out of drafts, to cool.

Label.

Store in cool, dry place.

2. WATER BATH. This method is used for whole fruits and acidic vegetables. Filled clean, hot jars are processed on a rack in a deep pot (with lid) covered with boiling water for a stated period of time. Most products preserved in a water bath canner have a one-year shelf life.

General directions for water bath canning: In a cooking pot large enough to hold the number of jars you are going to process completely submerged in water, bring water to a near boil. Place a rack on the bottom of the pot.

Fill clean, hot jars with prepared food to be preserved, leaving one-half-inch headspace in each filled jar (unless otherwise specified). Remove air bubbles from jars by pushing around edge of jar with a rubber spatula. Wipe sealing edges clean with a dry cloth. Place lid and cap on each jar and twist closed. Do not seal tightly.

Place jars on rack at the bottom of the pot, allowing free circulation of the boiling water around and under each jar. The water must be at least three inches above tops of jars (add water if necessary). Bring to a boil as quickly as possible. When water is at a vigorous boil, begin counting off the processing time necessary for the individual recipe.

When processing time is reached, using tongs, remove jars from boiling water bath. Complete the seal by tightening screw cap. Invert jars. (This will test for leaks.)

After about 10 minutes, set jars upright. Place about two inches apart on wire racks or newspaper, out of drafts, to cool. Label.

Store in a cool, dry place.

3. REFRIGERATOR. This method is generally used for foods that will be consumed quickly, either cooked or raw. There will be a few recipes that, due to either alcohol- or vinegar-based liquid, will have a long refrigeration life. However, unless otherwise specified, most refrigerated preserves will have a very short shelf life.

General directions for refrigerated gourmet preserves: Fill clean, hot containers with prepared food. Wipe sealing edges with a clean, dry cloth. Seal with an airtight cover.

If necessary, cool to room temperature.

Label.

Refrigerate. To speed cooling, place in coldest part of refrigerator for about three hours, with air space of at least one inch on all sides. Store in the refrigerator for no more than the suggested maxium storage period given in each recipe.

4. FREEZER. This method is used for anything except those foods (such as pickles) in which the freezing and thawing process will break down the texture, resulting in an unappealing product. Its success depends more than any other preserving method on the quality of the fresh fruit or vegetable. It must be *extremely fresh.* Frozen cooked foods have a shelf life of approximately 8 to 12 months.

General directions for frozen preserves: Fill sterilized containers with fresh cold foods. Remove as much air as possible from the container by turning a spatula around the edges and tamping down. Leave enough headspace for food to expand during the freezing process. Wipe sealing edges with a clean, dry cloth. Seal with an absolutely airtight lid.

Label.

Freeze immediately. It is essential that your freezer be at

least zero degrees Fahrenheit or below while the freezing process is taking place. An even temperature will ensure high quality. It is suggested that you do not overload your freezer when freezing gourmet preserves. Most manufacturers recommend that you add no more than two pounds per cubic foot of freezer space for quick freezing.

Each method has its use. In some recipes a choice will be given, in others only one method is suggested. In the latter case, please follow the suggestion for the best possible results. I re-iterate, *there are no shortcuts.*

Sealing Preserved Foods

Foods preserved by the open-kettle method may be sealed in two ways.

• A sterilized rubber-edged lid and screw cap are placed on the filled standard canning jar while both jar and filling are boiling hot. This will provide a tight vacuum seal. You should, when using this method, invert the sealed jar for a minute or two so that the heat can destroy any bacteria that may be on the lid.
Turn right side up to cool as directed on page 14.
• Any hot sterilized glass container is filled with hot food to one-half inch from the top. Edges are wiped clean with a dry cloth.
A one-eighth-inch layer of hot melted paraffin is imme-diately poured over the filling. (*Paraffin must cover the entire top and touch the edge of the container.*) Make certain that the paraffin seal has no bubbles that can allow air into the filling. Do not move containers until paraffin is hard.
Cover with a clean cap, either the mate to the container or aluminum foil or clear plastic wrap held in place by a rubber band.

Foods preserved by the water bath method will make their own vacuum seal during processing. Those preserved by refrig-eration or freezing are not usually vacuum-sealed, but they must

16

be stored in absolutely *airtight* lidded containers or in tightly sealed plastic bags.

PREPARATION OF CONTAINERS

Whether commercially available canning jars, reusable jars, plastic containers, or disposable plastic bags, all preserving containers must be *clean, free of any damage*, and *appealing to look at.*

Containers and lids (other than sealed plastic bags) must be washed in hot, soapy water and well rinsed in hot water before use.

If a sterile container is required, you must use one that can withstand the period of time required in a boiling water bath. Commercial canning jars are best suited for this.

To sterilize jars: In a large pot, cover jars and lids with hot water. Bring to a rapid boil and boil for 10 minutes. Remove from heat. Keep jars in water until ready to use. If water cools down, or for some reason you get interrupted, place pot back over the heat and bring to a boil again.

If recipe calls for a clean, hot container, wash and rinse as directed above. Cover jars and lids with boiling water. Keep them in hot water until ready to use.

Some home dishwashers are hot enough to use for the sterilization of jars. By all means, use one if you can. However, the jars still must be *hot* and *sterile* when filled.

LABELING AND STORING

If you are going to do a lot of preserving, it is nice to have the extra touch of a personalized label. You can purchase decorated labels from card shops or mail-order catalogs, or if you buy standard canning jars they are included in the carton. You can also have a label printed with your name as well as a spot for the date, shelf life, and contents. Any neighborhood printer should be able to help you select an appropriate style.

If you want to keep labeling simple, you can purchase sheets of gummed labels or roll labels from a stationery store and hand-write or type the necessary information on each one.

No matter how you choose to do it, *you must label!* List the *date, shelf life,* and *contents* on *each* jar or container. Uniform labeling, about two inches from the bottom of the container, will make your stacked jars look very attractive.

All recipes will have specific storing directions. Some will require refrigeration, while a few might be suitable for freezing also. In each case, the individual recipe will make note of these possibilities. In this instance, follow normal refrigeration and freezer precautions.

For maximum results, store all canned foods in a cool, dark place for no longer than one year. Foods may be stored longer, but occasionally the color and the taste will begin to fade.

PRESENTATION

You don't have to shout, "I made it myself!" if you take care to present your homemade preserves with the same attention you gave to making them.

If you label each container with an attractive sticker, you will not need much more. However, canning jars seem to lend themselves to caps cut from pretty fabric prints. Cut a circle of fabric about one inch larger in diameter than the lid (pinking shears give you an even more attractive edge). Tie the circle around the cap with ribbon, colored cord, or cotton string. Be sure to choose colors that compliment the color of the contents.

If you want to use your stores for gift giving, you might wish to enhance them either with a compatible homemade gift, such as scones with Rhubarb Ginger Jam, or with a store-bought partner, Salsa Inferno and a hand-thrown Mexican pottery server.

Using your own homemade gourmet preserves can only add to your gourmet table. So many cooks make everything from scratch and then use purchased jams, sauces, or other condiments. A simple grilled hamburger (and not one grilled over a mesquite fire) becomes a gourmand's treat when served with homemade Blueberry Catsup or Red Pepper Mustard. And you certainly wouldn't serve a commercial syrup over homemade ice cream.

Presentation is in the eye of both the maker and beholder. Use your culinary skill to its best advantage. Package your goods in beautiful containers and use them to intensify the fine taste of your gourmet meals.

2

Jellies, Jams, and Preserves

Jellies, jams, and preserves differ only in texture, and although different *they all must gel.* Each has the same four basic components: fruit for flavor; sugar for preserving, sweetness, and consistency; acid for thickening; and pectin for jelling. Jelly will be a clear, soft, solid mass, while jams and preserves are full-fruited and can be either runny or firm depending on your preference.

The fruit in each should be of the highest quality and of uniform ripeness. (An exception to this is if you are not using commercial pectin, in which case the ratio of ripe to underripe fruit should be four to one.) Discard that which shows signs of bruising or spoilage. Remove stems. For jams and preserves, core, seed, and peel (unless using seeds and peels for pectin). For jelly, cook entire fruit for its juice. Prepare as directed in individual recipes.

I have not had much success using substitutes for white sugar. I have found that honey can replace no more than one-quarter of the amount of sugar called for in any individual recipe. Cane or beet sugar can be used interchangeably.

Fresh lemon juice or cider or apple vinegars are the usual added acids. Tart or underripe apples, crab apples, cranberries, tart grapes, blackberries, and plums do not require additional acid for thickening, but lemon or grapefruit juice is frequently added to enhance the flavor.

Most of the recipes I use call for commercial pectin. I have recently begun experimenting with Sure Gel Light Fruit Pectin made by the General Foods Corporation. It requires about one-third less sugar than other commercial pectins and gives you a fresher-tasting jam, jelly, or preserve. Unless otherwise stated, follow the directions on the brand of pectin you use.

If you choose to cook without commercial pectin, you must adjust the ratio of sugar to fruit.

Peels and cores contain much of the natural pectin in fruits, so retain them when possible. Tart apples are very high in natural pectin, therefore their juice may be used to supplement pectin in all other fruits.

Jellies are made from the juice of cooked fruits or vegetables, extracted by dripping it through a cloth jelly bag. Patience is required to make a sparkling clear jelly, as you may not squeeze or cajole juice through the bag or your jelly will be cloudy.

If you are not using commercial pectin, the juice is combined with sugar in the ratio of two-thirds cup sugar to one cup juice.

To extract juice from fruit and vegetables: Wash and dry the fruit or vegetable. Cut away all damaged parts. Cut fruit or vegetable into chunks. Do not peel or core (the exception to this is pineapple, which should be peeled).

Place fruit or vegetable in heavy kettle. Add one cup water for each quart of hard fruit (such as apples or cranberries). Soft fruits and berries should be gently crushed to get the juice flowing. (If additional liquid is necessary, try not to add more than one cup of water, to help prevent scorching.) Bring to a boil over high heat. Lower heat to medium, stirring frequently.

Hard fruit or vegetables will need approximately 30 minutes to extract juice, soft fruit and berries about 10 minutes. Do not overcook, as this will decrease the flavor and pectin. Remove from heat.

Pour food and juices into a wet jelly bag (or a colander lined with lightweight cotton or a double piece of cheesecloth) placed over a bowl or pot large enough to hold the dripping juice. Let drip for about 12 hours for clear juice. *Do not squeeze bag.* Use clear juice only. Discard all residue in the jelly bag.

Jams are made of crushed fruit. The fruit is combined with sugar in the proportion of one-half to two-thirds cup sugar to one cup fruit, if you are not using commercial pectin.

Preserves are made from berries, cherries, sliced or quartered fruit, cut up vegetables, or melon rinds. When not using commercial pectin, from three-quarters to one cup sugar to one cup fruit is used. Preserved fruits should retain their shape and be plump, clear, and tender.

My younger son calls me the expert at runny jelly, jam, and preserves. I say if it's runny it has more uses. A great excuse to cover failure but, in truth, an example of turning failure to your advantage. Runny jams or preserves make great dessert toppings, cake fillings, and meat sauce bases and can still be used on toast if you hold the slice flat. Runny jelly is perfect for glazes and dessert toppings, and, if you spread it on lightly, it won't even run off the edge of your bread.

All jellies, jams, and preserves are made by the open-kettle method and are vacuum sealed in canning jars with rubber-edged lids and caps or with melted paraffin, as described on page 16. They may also be refrigerated for short-term storage, and some may be frozen, if so directed in the recipe.

Jellies, Jams, and Preserves

JELLIES
Jalapeño Jelly • *Port Wine Jelly* • *Horseradish Jelly* • *Cassis Jelly* • *Herb or Mint Jellies* • *Orange Sauterne Jelly* • *Ginger Apple Jelly* • *Champagne Jelly*

JAMS
Framboise • *Spiced Tomato Jam* • *Maryella Mixon's Winter Blueberry Jam* • *Blackberry Brandy Jam* • *Fresh Fig Jam* • *Basil Jam* • *Pennsylvania Peach Jam* • *Strawberry Grand Marnier Jam* • *Annie McDonagh's Rhubarb Ginger Jam* • *Sambuca Romana Jam* • *Bar-le-Duc Jam*

PRESERVES
Mom's Special Strawberry Preserves • *Kumquat Grand Marnier Preserves* • *Shaker Green Tomato Preserves* • *Pure Raspberry Preserves* • *Black Forest Preserves* • *Papaya Lime Preserves* • *Ginger Pear Preserves*

Jalapeño Jelly

QUANTITY:
4 ½-pint jars
PRESERVING METHOD USED:
Open kettle
STORAGE:
Vacuum-sealed—1 year
Refrigerated—6 weeks

¾ cup chopped jalapeño (or
  serrano) peppers
2 medium green bell peppers,
  seeded and sliced
1½ cups distilled white vinegar
6½ cups sugar
1 6-ounce bottle liquid pectin
1 tablespoon dried red pepper
  flakes
Green food coloring (optional)

You can almost guarantee that Jalapeño Jelly will be served at some point during a visit to the American South. I'm not sure why, but this piquant, multipurpose jelly is a Southern favorite. It is generally used as an hors d'oeuvre with cream cheese on water biscuits. You can also use it as a glaze for meats, game, and poultry or as an accompaniment to meats or game.

Place jalapeño peppers, green peppers, and vinegar in bowl of food processor. Using metal blade and quick on-and-off turns, finely grind peppers. Scrape pepper mixture into heavy saucepan. Stir in sugar. Cook over high heat, stirring constantly, until liquid comes to a full, rolling boil. Boil for 10 minutes. Remove from heat. Stir in liquid pectin, red pepper flakes, and 2 to 3 drops food coloring, if desired. Immediately pour into hot sterilized jars and vacuum seal as directed on page 16.

Port Wine Jelly

Probably derived from the old English port wine dessert gelatin, Port Wine Jelly is a tasty addition to your gourmet preserves. It can be made from other rich red wines, and apple juice may be substituted for grape. It is used as a spread on scones, tea biscuits, English muffins, or tea breads and as a glaze for, or accompaniment to, pork dishes, chicken, or duck.

Place wine, juice, and sugar in heavy saucepan. Bring to a boil over medium heat. Stir constantly until sugar is completely dissolved. Remove from heat and stir in liquid pectin. Skim off foam with metal spoon and immediately pour into hot sterilized jars. Vacuum seal as directed on page 16.

QUANTITY:
4 ½-pint jars
PRESERVING METHOD USED:
Open kettle
STORAGE:
Vacuum-sealed—1 year
Refrigerated—6 weeks

1 cup port wine
1 cup fresh grape juice (see page 22), or fine-quality commercially canned grape juice
3½ cups sugar
½ 6-ounce bottle liquid pectin

Horseradish Jelly

QUANTITY:
3 ½-pint jars
PRESERVING METHOD USED:
Open kettle
STORAGE:
Vacuum-sealed—1 year
Refrigerated—6 weeks

1 cup grated fresh horseradish
1 cup white wine vinegar
¼ teaspoon minced fresh sage
3¼ cups sugar
½ cup liquid pectin

One of my favorite jellies and a fine old English recipe also used by the Shakers. This jelly is primarily used as a garnish for cold beef, meat salads, or pot roast.

Place horseradish, vinegar, sage, and sugar in heavy saucepan. Cook over high heat, stirring constantly, until mixture comes to a hard boil. Add liquid pectin and again bring to a full boil. Boil for 1 minute. Remove from heat and skim off foam with metal spoon. Immediately pour into hot sterilized jars and vacuum seal as directed on page 16.

Cassis Jelly

A perfect garnish for poultry and game. A gourmet replacement in all desserts, sauces, or glazes calling for currant jelly.

Place currant juice (or cranberry-apple juice), cassis, lemon juice, and sugar in heavy saucepan over high heat. Bring to a boil, stirring constantly. Add liquid pectin and, stirring constantly, cook until mixture comes to a full, rolling boil. Boil for 1 minute. Remove from heat and skim off foam with metal spoon. Immediately pour into hot sterilized jars and vacuum seal as directed on page 16.

QUANTITY:
4 ½-pint jars
PRESERVING METHOD USED:
Open kettle
STORAGE:
Vacuum-sealed—1 year
Refrigerated—6 weeks

3 cups fresh currant juice, or fresh cranberry-apple juice (see page 22), or fine-quality commercially canned unprocessed juice, strained
1 cup cassis
2 tablespoons lemon juice
3¼ cups sugar
½ 6-ounce bottle liquid pectin

Herb or Mint Jellies

QUANTITY:
4 ½-pint jars
PRESERVING METHOD USED:
Open kettle
STORAGE:
Vacuum-sealed—1 year
Refrigerated—6 weeks

1 cup finely chopped fresh
  mint (stems and leaves), or
  sage (stems and leaves), or
  marjoram (stems and
  leaves), or tarragon (stems
  and leaves), or basil (stems
  and leaves)
1 cup boiling water
1 teaspoon fresh lemon juice
3 cups sugar
½ cup cider vinegar
½ 6-ounce bottle liquid pectin
Green food coloring (optional)
4 sprigs of the herb used
  (optional)

Herb jellies are primarily used for meat or poultry garnish. I use them on tea sandwiches combined with a thin spread of sweet butter, fresh goat cheese, or other soft, pungent cheeses and pumpernickel bread.

In glass, heat-resistant bowl place chopped fresh mint or herb. Add 1 cup boiling water. Cover and let stand for 30 minutes. Strain liquid through cheesecloth and add enough water to make 1 cup. Place herb infusion, lemon juice, sugar, and vinegar in heavy saucepan. Cook over high heat until mixture comes to a boil. Immediately add liquid pectin and food coloring, if desired, and continue cooking until mixture comes to a full, rolling boil. Boil for exactly 1 minute. Remove from heat and skim off foam with metal spoon. Immediately pour into hot sterilized jars, add optional sprigs of herbs, if desired, and vacuum seal as directed on page 16.

28

Orange Sauterne Jelly

Sauterne may be replaced by other white wines in this sweet-tart jelly. The flavor lends itself for use both as a spread on breads and as a meat glaze. It can also be reheated for use as a dessert sauce on ice cream, sliced oranges, or berries.

Place orange juice, sauterne, and lemon juice in heavy saucepan. Mix together ¾ cup sugar and the powdered light fruit pectin. Add to wine mixture. Cook over high heat, stirring constantly, until mixture comes to a hard boil. Stir in remaining sugar. Bring to a rolling boil, stirring constantly. Boil for 1 minute. Remove from heat and skim off foam with metal spoon. Immediately pour into hot sterilized jars, add optional sprigs of tarragon, if desired, and vacuum seal as directed on page 16.

QUANTITY:
6 ½-pint jars
PRESERVING METHOD USED:
Open kettle
STORAGE:
Vacuum-sealed—1 year
Refrigerated—6 weeks

3½ cups fresh orange juice, strained
1½ cups good-quality sauterne
1 teaspoon fresh lemon juice
3¼ cups sugar
1 box powdered light fruit pectin
6 sprigs of fresh tarragon (optional)

Ginger Apple Jelly

QUANTITY:
5 ½-pint jars
PRESERVING METHOD USED:
Open kettle
STORAGE:
Vacuum-sealed—1 year
Refrigerated—6 weeks

4 cups fresh apple juice (see
   page 22), or fine-quality
   commercially canned
   unprocessed apple juice,
   strained
3 tablespoons grated fresh
   ginger
1 teaspoon fresh lemon juice
3 cups sugar
1 box powdered light fruit
   pectin

A special tangy jelly used as a replacement for the multi-purpose apple jelly in sauces, desserts, and glazes.

Place apple juice and ginger in heavy saucepan over high heat. Bring to a boil. Immediately remove from heat, cover, and let stand for 1 hour. Strain to remove ginger particles. Add lemon juice. Place juice in heavy saucepan over high heat. Mix together ¾ cup sugar and the powdered light fruit pectin. Add to juice. Cook over high heat, stirring constantly, until mixture comes to a hard boil. Stir in remaining sugar. Bring to a rolling boil, stirring constantly. Boil for 1 minute. Immediately remove from heat, skim off foam with metal spoon, and pour into hot sterilized jars. Vacuum seal as directed on page 16.

Champagne Jelly

A wonderful bite to spread on tea breads, scones, or biscuits. A superb coating on white or pound cake, to be covered with a bittersweet chocolate glaze. Or try it as a glaze on broiled fruits for a brunch treat.

Place champagne, lemon juice, and powdered pectin in heavy saucepan over high heat. Cook, stirring constantly, until mixture comes to a boil. Immediately add sugar. Cook, stirring constantly, until mixture reaches a full, rolling boil. Immediately remove from heat, skim off foam with metal spoon, and pour into hot sterilized jars. Vacuum seal as directed on page 16.

QUANTITY:
4 ½-pint jars
PRESERVING METHOD USED:
Open kettle
STORAGE:
Vacuum-sealed—1 year
Refrigerated—6 weeks

2 cups very good champagne
1 teaspoon lemon juice
2 tablespoons powdered pectin
3 cups sugar

Framboise

QUANTITY:
4 ½-pint jars
PRESERVING METHOD USED:
Open kettle
STORAGE:
Vacuum-sealed—1 year
Refrigerated—6 weeks

4½ cups fresh raspberries
3 cups sugar
¼ cup framboise

The combination of the delicacy of fresh raspberries and the mellow framboise (raspberry brandy) makes a truly remarkable jam. Use both as a spread and as a dessert garnish.

Place all ingredients in heavy saucepan over medium heat. Bring to a boil, stirring occasionally. When mixture comes to a boil, raise heat to high and cook, stirring constantly, for about 20 minutes. As mixture begins to thicken, watch carefully to prevent sticking. When mixture has reached a jamlike consistency, immediately remove from heat. Pour into hot sterilized jars and vacuum seal as directed on page 16.

Spiced Tomato Jam

This jam was an early American favorite—a way to use the bounty of the August tomato crop. Spiced tomato jam can also be made with green, yellow, or plum tomatoes and may be used both as a spread and as a glaze or as an accompaniment to meat or poultry.

Mix together ¾ cup sugar and the powdered light fruit pectin. Add to tomatoes and all other ingredients, except cinnamon sticks and remaining sugar, in heavy saucepan over high heat. Cook, stirring constantly, until mixture comes to a hard boil. Stir in remaining sugar. Bring to a rolling boil, stirring constantly. Boil for 1 minute. Remove from heat and skim off foam with metal spoon. Immediately pour into hot sterilized jars, add 1 cinnamon stick per jar, and vacuum seal as directed on page 16.

QUANTITY:
4 ½-pint jars
PRESERVING METHOD USED:
Open kettle
STORAGE:
Vacuum-sealed—1 year
Refrigerated—6 weeks

3½ cups peeled and chopped fresh, ripe tomatoes, or canned tomatoes, drained and chopped
3 teaspoons fresh lemon juice
Grated rind of 1 lemon
½ teaspoon ground cinnamon
¼ teaspoon ground mace
¼ teaspoon ground ginger
3 cups sugar
1 box powdered light fruit pectin
4 cinnamon sticks

Maryella Mixon's Winter Blueberry Jam

QUANTITY:
4 ½-pint jars
PRESERVING METHOD USED:
Open kettle
STORAGE:
Vacuum-sealed—1 year
Refrigerated—6 weeks

1 cup chopped tart green
  apples (such as Granny
  Smith)
1 lemon, seeded and chopped
1 pint frozen fresh blueberries
3 cups sugar
½ cup water

Maryella Mixon has provided me with many wonderful recipes. Her fine Southern hospitality is renowned, and her table groans with fine food. This is her way of bringing summer to the winter table (blueberries being one fruit that freezes beautifully).

Place apples and lemon in bowl of food processor. Using metal blade and quick on-and-off turns, finely chop. Place all ingredients in large saucepan. Bring to a boil, stirring constantly, until blueberries thaw and sugar dissolves. Boil gently, uncovered, stirring occasionally, for about 30 minutes. When jam has thickened, remove from heat. Immediately pour into hot sterilized jars and vacuum seal as directed on page 16.

Blackberry Brandy Jam

A perfect blending of fresh blackberries and brandy. This may be used whenever a fine preserve is required as a spread or with desserts.

Combine blackberries, lemon juice, and sugar in heavy saucepan over medium heat. Bring to a boil, stirring frequently. Raise heat and cook, stirring constantly, for about 20 minutes. Add brandy. Cook for an additional 10 minutes, or until mixture begins to thicken. Remove from heat and skim off foam with metal spoon. Immediately pour into hot sterilized jars and vacuum seal as directed on page 16.

QUANTITY:
4 ½-pint jars
PRESERVING METHOD USED:
Open kettle
STORAGE:
Vacuum-sealed—1 year
Refrigerated—6 weeks

4½ cups fresh blackberries
3 teaspoons fresh lemon juice
3 cups sugar
¼ cup blackberry brandy

Fresh Fig Jam

QUANTITY:
4 1/2-pint jars
PRESERVING METHOD USED:
Open kettle
STORAGE:
Vacuum-sealed—1 year
Refrigerated—6 weeks

4 cups chopped fresh figs
1/4 cup fresh lemon juice
Grated rind of 1 lemon
1/2 cup water
1/4 teaspoon ground cinnamon
3 cups sugar

I generally have difficulty gathering enough figs to make jam, as ripe figs and cheese are about my most favorite meal. Whenever you can gather enough to make this jam, do so. Not only is it a great spread, it is a perfect filling for cookies and cakes.

Place all ingredients in heavy saucepan over medium heat. Bring to a boil, stirring frequently. When mixture has reached the boiling point, raise heat and cook for approximately 20 minutes, stirring frequently, until mixture has thickened. Watch to prevent scorching. Remove from heat. Immediately pour into hot sterilized jars and vacuum seal as directed on page 16.

Basil Jam

A new twist to an old favorite. This pungent jam can be used as a spread as well as an accompaniment to meats and poultry.

Mix ¾ cup sugar and the powdered light fruit pectin together. Add to tomatoes, basil, and lemon juice in heavy saucepan. Bring mixture to a full, rolling boil over high heat, stirring constantly. Add remaining sugar. Bring mixture again to a full, rolling boil. Boil, stirring constantly, for 1 minute. Immediately remove from heat and skim off foam with metal spoon. Pour at once into hot sterilized jars and vacuum seal as directed on page 16.

QUANTITY:
4 ½-pint jars
PRESERVING METHOD USED:
Open kettle
STORAGE:
Vacuum-sealed—1 year
Refrigerated—6 weeks

3½ cups cooked, seeded, and chopped fresh tomatoes
¾ cup chopped fresh basil (stems and leaves)
¼ cup lemon juice
3 cups sugar
1 box powdered light fruit pectin

Pennsylvania Peach Jam

QUANTITY:
6 ½-pint jars
PRESERVING METHOD USED:
Open kettle
STORAGE:
Vacuum-sealed—1 year
Refrigerated—6 weeks

4 cups chopped fresh peaches
1 teaspoon lemon juice
1½ cups fresh orange juice
Grated rind of 1 orange
1 bottle maraschino cherries,
    drained and cut in half
3 cups sugar
1 box powdered light fruit
    pectin

I don't know why this is called Pennsylvania Peach Jam, but I assume it was devised by the wonderful folks in the Pennsylvania Dutch country.

Mix together ¾ cup sugar and the powdered light fruit pectin. Add to other ingredients, except remaining sugar. Cook over high heat, stirring constantly, until mixture comes to a hard boil. Stir in remaining sugar. Bring to a rolling boil, stirring constantly. Boil for 1 minute. Remove from heat and skim off foam with metal spoon. Immediately pour into hot sterilized jars and vacuum seal as directed on page 16.

Strawberry Grand Marnier Jam

This is a wonderful jam to use as a jelly roll filling and, of course, as a spread on all tea breads, scones, and muffins.

Place strawberries and sugar in heavy saucepan over medium heat. Bring to a boil, stirring constantly. Raise heat and cook for about 30 minutes, or until mixture reaches a jamlike consistency. Remove from heat. Stir in Grand Marnier. Immediately pour into hot sterilized jars and vacuum seal as directed on page 16.

QUANTITY:
4 ½-pint jars
PRESERVING METHOD USED:
Open kettle
STORAGE:
Vacuum-sealed—1 year
Refrigerated—6 weeks

4½ cups fresh strawberries
3 cups sugar
¼ cup Grand Marnier

Annie McDonagh's Rhubarb Ginger Jam

QUANTITY:
5 ½-pint jars
PRESERVING METHOD USED:
Open kettle
STORAGE:
Vacuum-sealed—1 year
Refrigerated—6 weeks

4 cups cooked, chopped
  rhubarb (see page 9)
1 tablespoon grated fresh
  ginger
1 tablespoon fresh lemon juice
¼ cup peeled and chopped
  ginger (you can also use
  candied ginger, if you wish
  a less pungent flavor)
4 cups sugar
1 box powdered light fruit
  pectin

Both rhubarb and ginger were early American favorites brought from the British Isles, where the zesty flavor of ginger was (and still is) used frequently as a dessert enhancer. (Rhubarb has historically been a favorite English and Irish dessert fruit.) This recipe was given to me by my Irish-speakin' friend, Annie McDonagh.

Mix together ¾ cup sugar and the powdered light fruit pectin. Add to rhubarb, grated ginger, and lemon juice. Stir to mix. Place in heavy saucepan over high heat, stirring constantly, until mixture comes to a hard boil. Stir in remaining sugar. Bring to a rolling boil, stirring constantly, for 1 minute. Remove from heat. Add peeled, chopped ginger. Stir. Skim off foam with metal spoon. Immediately pour into hot sterilized jars and vacuum seal as directed on page 16.

40

Sambuca Romana Jam

You'll have to remember the coffee beans, which give the finished jam its special taste. It makes a dramatic topping on lemon sorbet with the beans to be nibbled with espresso.

QUANTITY:
4 ½-pint jars
PRESERVING METHOD USED:
Open kettle
STORAGE:
Vacuum-sealed—1 year
Refrigerated—6 weeks

Mix ¾ cup sugar and the powdered light fruit pectin together. Stir into blueberries, lemon rind, water, and Sambuca in a heavy saucepan. Cook over high heat, stirring constantly, until mixture comes to a hard boil. Stir in remaining sugar. Bring to a rolling boil, still stirring constantly. Boil for 1 minute. Remove from heat. Skim off foam with metal spoon. Place 10 coffee beans in each jar. Immediately pour jam into hot sterilized jars and vacuum seal as directed on page 16.

5 cups crushed, fresh
  blueberries
1 teaspoon grated fresh lemon
  rind
½ cup water
½ cup Sambuca Romana
2½ cups sugar
1 box powdered light fruit
  pectin
10 coffee beans per jar

Bar-le-Duc Jam

QUANTITY:
5 ½-pint jars
PRESERVING METHOD USED:
Open kettle
STORAGE:
Vacuum-sealed—1 year
Refrigerated—6 weeks

8 *cups whole red currants*
1 *tablespoon fresh lemon juice*
6 *cups sugar*

Named for the town in France that is famous for its red currant jams, this is the jam most frequently called for in fine French cooking.

Place currants, lemon juice, and 4 cups sugar in heavy saucepan over medium heat. Bring to a boil, stirring frequently. Cook for 5 minutes, stirring constantly. Remove from heat, cover, and let stand in a cool place for 12 hours. Then place over medium heat and add remaining sugar. Cook, stirring constantly, until sugar dissolves. Raise heat and bring to a full, rolling boil, then lower heat for a low boil. Stirring frequently, cook for about 30 minutes, or until jam is thick. Immediately pour into hot sterilized jars and vacuum seal as directed on page 16.

Mom's Special Strawberry Preserves

Year after year, my mother made these old-fashioned preserves. A bit sweet for today's taste, but as simple, as pure, and as old a recipe as you can find.

Mix berries and sugar together in glass bowl. Cover and let stand overnight. In the morning, place berry mixture in heavy saucepan over medium heat. Add lemon juice. Bring to a full, rolling boil. Boil for 5 minutes, stirring constantly. Remove from heat. Cover and let stand in a cool place for 24 hours. Again bring to a boil. Remove from heat and immediately pour into hot sterilized jars. Vacuum seal as directed on page 16.

QUANTITY:
4 ½-pint jars
PRESERVING METHOD USED:
Open kettle
STORAGE:
Vacuum-sealed—1 year
Refrigerated—6 weeks

1 quart medium-sized very ripe, fresh strawberries
4 cups sugar
½ cup lemon juice

Kumquat Grand Marnier Preserves

QUANTITY:
4 ½-pint jars
PRESERVING METHOD USED:
Open kettle
STORAGE:
Vacuum-sealed—1 year
Refrigerated—6 weeks

4½ cups whole kumquats
2 teaspoons salt
3½ cups sugar
1 cup clover honey
3 cups fresh orange juice
½ cup water
¼ cup Grand Marnier

This is technically a marmalade, since you use the whole kumquat, but it is known throughout the South as a special winter preserve. I use it most frequently as an accompaniment to game.

With a sterilized needle, make about 6 punctures in the skin of each kumquat. Place in glass bowl. Cover with 2 quarts water and 2 teaspoons salt. Cover and set aside for at least 12 hours. Drain. Rinse with fresh water and add all remaining ingredients. Bring to a boil in heavy saucepan over medium heat. Cook for approximately 40 minutes, or until mixture begins to be clear and quite thick. Remove from heat. Cover and let stand for 2 days. Again bring to a boil. Remove from heat and immediately pour into hot sterilized jars. Vacuum seal as directed on page 16.

Shaker Green Tomato Preserves

Updated to gel with less sugar than the preserve made by the Shakers, this has long been an American favorite. It is a perfect use for late fall tomatoes.

Place chopped green tomatoes and salt, with water to cover, in glass bowl. Cover and soak for at least 6 hours. Drain and rinse with fresh water. Place chopped tomatoes, lemon, and spices in heavy saucepan over medium heat. Mix ¾ cup sugar with the powdered light fruit pectin. Add to tomato mixture. Cook over high heat, stirring constantly, until mixture comes to a hard boil. Stir in remaining sugar. Bring to a rolling boil, stirring constantly. Boil for 1 minute. Remove from heat. Skim off foam with metal spoon. Immediately pour into hot sterilized jars and vacuum seal as directed on page 16.

QUANTITY:
4 ½-pint jars
PRESERVING METHOD USED:
Open kettle
STORAGE:
Vacuum-sealed—1 year
Refrigerated—6 weeks

3¼ cups chopped green tomatoes
1 teaspoon salt
1 lemon, seeded and chopped fine
2 tablespoons chopped preserved ginger
1 teaspoon ground cinnamon
¼ teaspoon ground nutmeg
¼ teaspoon ground allspice
1½ cups brown sugar
1 box powdered light fruit pectin

Pure Raspberry Preserves

QUANTITY:
8 ½-pint jars
PRESERVING METHOD USED:
Open kettle
STORAGE:
Vacuum-sealed—1 year
Refrigerated—6 weeks

9 cups firm whole raspberries
1 tablespoon fresh lemon juice
4½ cups sugar
1 box powdered light fruit
    pectin

Our family favorite and, judging from all the requests I get, a favorite of our friends—although my husband often wonders if the miles we drive to buy flats of fresh, perfect raspberries at an affordable price are really worth the difference in my canning budget. Yet, we do it year after year.

Mix ¾ cup sugar with the powdered light fruit pectin. Add to raspberries and lemon juice in heavy saucepan. Over high heat quickly bring fruit mixture to a full boil, stirring constantly. Add remaining sugar. Continue to stir and bring to a full, rolling boil. Boil hard for 1 minute, stirring constantly. Remove from heat and immediately pour into hot sterilized jars. Vacuum seal as directed on page 16.

Black Forest Preserves

A wonderful dessert topping or filling for a homemade Black Forest cake. A special brunch treat when spread on toasted fresh rye bread.

Mix ¾ cup sugar with the powdered light fruit pectin. Add to cherries, lemon juice, and kirschwasser in heavy saucepan. Bring to a boil over medium heat, stirring constantly. When mixture comes to a hard boil, stir in remaining sugar. Bring to a full, rolling boil, stirring constantly. Boil for 1 minute. Remove from heat. Skim off foam with metal spoon. Immediately pour into hot sterilized jars and vacuum seal as directed on page 16.

QUANTITY:
6 ½-pint jars
PRESERVING METHOD USED:
Open kettle
STORAGE:
Vacuum-sealed—1 year
Refrigerated—6 weeks

4½ cups pitted and halved
    fresh Bing cherries
1 teaspoon fresh lemon juice
¼ cup kirschwasser
3¼ cups sugar
1 box powdered light fruit
    pectin

Papaya Lime Preserves

QUANTITY:
4 ½-pint jars
PRESERVING METHOD USED:
Open kettle
STORAGE:
Vacuum-sealed—1 year
Refrigerated—6 weeks

2 cups water
2 cups sugar
¼ cup lime juice
Grated rind of 1 lime
¼ teaspoon ground cinnamon
2 cups peeled, seeded, and
    chunked fresh papaya

The first exotic fruit I ever tasted in my first grown-up, fancy restaurant, papaya and lime combined make an unforgettable flavor. Papaw may be used to replace papaya if it is native to your area.

Combine water, sugar, lime juice, rind, and cinnamon in heavy saucepan over medium heat. Bring to a boil and boil rapidly for 5 minutes. Add papaya. Bring to a boil. Lower heat and cook slowly for about 40 minutes, or until fruit is transparent. Remove from heat and immediately pour into hot sterilized jars. Vacuum seal as directed on page 16.

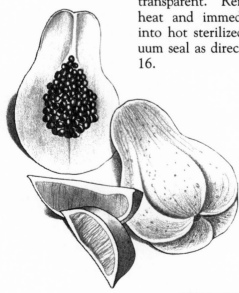

Ginger Pear Preserves

I like to use this preserve mixed with whipped cream on fresh, warm gingerbread. It also makes a wonderful glaze on baked winter fruits.

Mix all ingredients together in heavy saucepan. Bring to a boil. Cook gently for about 15 minutes. Remove from heat, cover, and let stand in a cool place for 12 hours. Again bring to a boil over high heat. Cook, stirring constantly, for about 40 minutes, or until thick and translucent. Remove from heat and immediately pour into hot sterilized jars. Vacuum seal as directed on page 16.

QUANTITY:
5 ½-pint jars
PRESERVING METHOD USED:
Open kettle
STORAGE:
Vacuum-sealed—1 year
Refrigerated—6 weeks

6 cups cored and chunked hard, ripe pears
1 whole lemon, seeded and chopped
¼ cup grated fresh ginger (or chopped candied ginger, if preferred)
¼ cup Poire William
4 cups sugar
½ cup water

3

Conserves, Marmalades, and Butters

Conserves are made of combinations of several fruits or vegetables and usually contain nuts and raisins. They are cooked until thick and clear and of the consistency of jelly. Conserves are generally used as a condiment for meats or game.

Marmalades are made of thinly sliced or chopped fruits or vegetables and will usually contain some rind. The fruits or vegetables are combined with a relatively large proportion of sugar. Marmalades should also be cooked until the pieces of fruit or vegetable are clear and the mixture is the consistency of jelly. When using citrus fruit, always use some of the white pith, as it is high in pectin. It is also important to try to use thin-skinned, untreated fruit, as it is much closer to its historical counterpart. Marmalades are used on tea breads, toast, scones, muffins, and as dessert toppings, and can also be used for glazing poultry, game, or pork.

Butters are made of fruit that has been cooked until tender in just enough water to prevent sticking. The cooked fruit is run through a food processor or sieve and then usually combined with sugar. Spices are occasionally added for a robust flavor. A fruit butter is cooked slowly and stirred frequently until very thick. Butters are the purest form of cooked fruit and can be made with no sugar, if desired. One of my favorite uses of butters is as a coating on duck. The crisp, succulent skin is especially delicious with a crackling fruit butter coating.

All conserves and marmalades are made by the open-kettle method and vacuum sealed either in canning jars with rubber-edged lids and caps or with hot paraffin as directed on page 16.

Most butters require a boiling water bath. If making them without the addition of any sugar, you will always have to process the jars in a 10-minute boiling water bath as described on page 14.

All may be refrigerated for short-term storage or frozen for a period of no longer than 12 months.

Conserves, Marmalades, and Butters

CONSERVES
Brandied Date Conserve • Cranberry Orange Conserve • Hot Tomato Conserve • Gumbo • Old Rummy • Basil Conserve

MARMALADES
Red Onion Marmalade • Microwave Marmalade • Carrot Marmalade • Our Marmalade • Grand Marnier Marmalade • Pumpkin Ginger Marmalade

BUTTERS
Apple Brandy Butter • Perfect Apple Butter • Bourbon Butter • Ginger Pear Butter

Brandied Date Conserve

A perfect filling—stirred into whipped cream—for cakes and sandwich cookies; a tasty topping for light cakes; and, of course, a nice, rich garnish for meats and game, particularly pork.

QUANTITY:
4 ½-pint jars
PRESERVING METHOD USED:
Open kettle
STORAGE:
Vacuum-sealed—1 year
Refrigerated—6 weeks
May be frozen

Combine dates, currants, brown sugar, orange juice, lemon juice, and water in heavy saucepan over medium heat. Bring to a boil. Lower heat and cook, stirring frequently, for 5 minutes. Remove from heat and stir in brandy and nuts. Immediately pour into hot sterilized jars and vacuum seal as directed on page 16.

2½ cups chopped dates
2 cups dried currants
1 cup brown sugar
½ cup fresh orange juice
3 tablespoons fresh lemon juice
½ cup water
½ cup very good brandy
½ cup chopped walnuts (or whatever nut you prefer)

Cranberry Orange Conserve

QUANTITY:
6 ½-pint jars
PRESERVING METHOD USED:
Open kettle
STORAGE:
Vacuum-sealed—1 year
Refrigerated—6 weeks
May be frozen

1 whole orange, seeded and
    finely chopped
1½ cups white sugar
1 cup fresh orange juice
4 cups whole cranberries
1 cup brown sugar
1 cup raisins
1½ cups chopped pecans

Always on our table at Thanksgiving and Christmas, but a tasty garnish for meats, poultry, and game all year long. I like to add a cup of Cranberry Orange Conserve to the batter when I make a pound cake.

Cook chopped orange, white sugar, and orange juice in heavy saucepan over medium heat for approximately 20 minutes, or until orange peel is soft. Add cranberries, brown sugar, and raisins. Cook until mixture comes to a boil, stirring frequently. Lower heat and cook at a low boil for about 10 minutes, stirring constantly, until mixture thickens. Remove from heat and stir in pecans. Immediately pour into hot sterilized jars and vacuum seal as directed on page 16.

Hot Tomato Conserve

A touch of Tex-Mex flavors updates this old-fashioned red tomato conserve. I invented this when I had too many yellow tomatoes (purchased at a bargain price, of course). We love it. Yellow tomatoes have a delicate flavor all their own, and it is only enhanced by the peppers.

Place all ingredients, except pumpkin seeds, in heavy saucepan over medium heat. Bring to a boil, stirring frequently. Lower heat, cover, and let simmer for about 1 hour, stirring frequently to prevent sticking. When mixture has thickened, remove from heat, stir in toasted pumpkin seeds, and immediately pour into hot sterilized jars. Vacuum seal as directed on page 16.

QUANTITY:
4 ½-pint jars
PRESERVING METHOD USED:
Open kettle
STORAGE:
Vacuum-sealed—1 year
Refrigerated—6 weeks
May be frozen

5 cups halved small yellow
   tomatoes
1 whole lemon, seeded and
   finely chopped
2 jalapeño (or serrano)
   peppers, seeded and finely
   chopped
1 cup white raisins
1 tablespoon grated fresh
   orange rind
1 cup light brown sugar
1 cup white sugar
½ cup butter
1 cup toasted pumpkin seeds
   (pepitas)

Gumbo

QUANTITY:
6 ½-pint jars
PRESERVING METHOD USED:
Open kettle
STORAGE:
Vacuum-sealed—1 year
Refrigerated—1 month
May be frozen

5 cups chopped, pitted plums
2 cups chopped and seeded
  whole oranges
1 cup white or dark raisins
1 tablespoon fresh lemon juice
½ teaspoon ground cinnamon
¼ teaspoon ground cloves
3 cups light brown sugar
1 cup whole nut pieces

Why plum conserves are called gumbo in most recipes I don't know. It is delicious, however, both as a dessert and as a meat accompaniment.

Plums and oranges may be chopped together in bowl of food processor, using metal blade. Combine all ingredients except nut meats in heavy saucepan over medium heat. Bring to a boil, stirring frequently. Cook at a low boil for about 20 minutes, stirring frequently to prevent scorching. When mixture has thickened, remove from heat, stir in nut meats, and immediately pour into hot sterilized jars. Vacuum seal as directed on page 16.

Old Rummy

A family favorite. We first made this with fresh fruit while vacationing in the Caribbean. Piña coladas are, of course, its inspiration. It makes a great base for homemade ice cream!

Combine all ingredients in heavy saucepan over medium heat. Bring to a boil. Lower heat and cook for 20 minutes. Remove from heat and immediately pour into hot sterilized jars. Vacuum seal as directed on page 16.

QUANTITY:
4 ½-pint jars
PRESERVING METHOD USED:
Open kettle
STORAGE:
Vacuum-sealed—1 year
Refrigerated—2 months
May be frozen

1 large fresh pineapple, peeled and chopped
1 cup grated fresh coconut
1 whole lemon, seeded and chopped
1 whole orange, seeded and chopped
1 cup good white wine
4 cups sugar

Basil Conserve

QUANTITY:
4 ½-pint jars
PRESERVING METHOD USED:
Open kettle
STORAGE:
Vacuum-sealed—1 year
Refrigerated—6 weeks
May be frozen

4 cups chopped green tomatoes
3 cups chopped fresh basil
  (stems and leaves)
1 cup dry white wine
1 whole lemon, seeded and
  chopped
3 cups sugar
1½ cups toasted pine nuts

I can never have too much basil. I use every piece I can get: The large woody plants go into flower arrangements, and my sauté pan gets the new tender shoots with garlic and oil for use on pasta. This conserve is absolutely wonderful with grilled meats and fish.

Combine all ingredients, except pine nuts, in heavy saucepan over medium heat. Bring to a boil. Lower heat and simmer for about 30 minutes, stirring frequently. When mixture has begun to thicken, remove from heat, stir in toasted pine nuts, and immediately pour into hot sterilized jars. Vacuum seal as directed on page 16.

GOURMET PRESERVES

Red Onion Marmalade

I clipped this recipe from a magazine (which one is long forgotten) to use for a cookout featuring grilled lime-marinated pork. It was such a hit that I have since expanded and added to it, and it is always on my winter preserves shelf.

Place onion, shallots, and sugar in heavy saucepan over low heat, stirring frequently until mixture begins to caramelize and turn a light brown color. Stir in all other ingredients. Cook over low heat, stirring frequently to prevent scorching, for about 45 minutes, or until mixture is a thick syrup. Immediately remove from heat and pour into hot sterilized jars. Vacuum seal as directed on page 16.

QUANTITY:
4 ½-pint jars
PRESERVING METHOD USED:
Open kettle
STORAGE:
Vacuum-sealed—1 year
Refrigerated—6 weeks
May be frozen

8 cups peeled, quartered, and sliced red onions
½ cup peeled and chopped shallots
½ cup light brown sugar
½ cup orange blossom honey
¼ cup red wine vinegar
1 cup dry red wine
¼ cup virgin olive oil
1 tablespoon chopped fresh sage
1 tablespoon fresh ground black pepper

Microwave Marmalade

QUANTITY:
About 1 cup
PRESERVING METHOD USED:
Microwave oven
STORAGE:
Refrigerated—for up to 1 week

*1 large seeded orange (or 1
large grapefruit, or 2 large
lemons, or 2 large limes, all
seeded)*
Sugar to equal fruit

I got this recipe from a reader's forum in a national food magazine. I can't remember which one, but I do thank her. I've made it from all kinds of citrus fruit. It really works. And it is certainly the quickest and easiest preserve I've ever come across.

Shred orange (or grapefruit, lemons, or limes) in bowl of food processor, using metal blade and quick on-and-off turns. Measure exactly and turn into a microwave bowl. Measure equal amount of white sugar and add to orange. Stir to mix. Place in center of microwave oven. Cook on medium, stirring twice, for about 6 minutes, or until syrup thickens. Do not overcook. Remove from oven, pour into sterilized container, cover, and refrigerate until ready to use.

Carrot Marmalade

This is the first traditional Shaker recipe I ever tried. I think that it is delicious used as both a spread and a glaze.

Place all ingredients in heavy saucepan over medium heat. Bring to a boil, stirring frequently. Lower heat and simmer slowly for about 30 minutes. When mixture begins to gel, remove from heat and immediately pour into hot sterilized jars. Vacuum seal as directed on page 16.

QUANTITY:
5 ½-pint jars
PRESERVING METHOD USED:
Open kettle
STORAGE:
Vacuum-sealed—1 year
Refrigerated—1 month
May be frozen

3 cups cooked, chopped carrots
2 whole lemons, seeded and chopped
1 whole orange, seeded and chopped
1 tablespoon ground cinnamon
4 cups sugar

Our Marmalade

QUANTITY:
6 ½-pint jars
PRESERVING METHOD USED:
Open kettle
STORAGE:
Vacuum-sealed—1 year
Refrigerated—6 weeks

My Scottish grandmother made it, my mother made it, and I make it. Its simplicity makes it truly a gourmet preserve.

Measure chopped fruit and place in heavy saucepan. Measure equal amounts of water and pour into saucepan. Bring to a boil. Lower heat and simmer for about 5 minutes. Remove from heat, cover, and let stand in a cool place for 24 hours. Again bring to a boil and cook over high heat for 10 minutes. Remove from heat, cover, and let stand in a cool place for another 24 hours. Measure out fruit mixture. Add equal amount of sugar. Again bring to a boil over medium heat. Cook, stirring constantly, for another 15 minutes, or until mixture begins to gel. Remove from heat and immediately pour into hot sterilized jars. Vacuum seal as directed on page 16.

3 *whole oranges, seeded and chopped*
3 *whole lemons, seeded and chopped*
Water to equal chopped fruit
Sugar to equal cooked fruit

Grand Marnier Marmalade

QUANTITY:
6 1/2-pint jars
PRESERVING METHOD USED:
Open kettle
STORAGE:
Vacuum-sealed—1 year
Refrigerated—2 months

2 cups thinly sliced kumquats
2 cups seeded and chopped
    whole navel oranges
7 cups water
1 teaspoon grated fresh lemon
    rind
3/4 cup Grand Marnier
Sugar to equal cooked fruit

A wonderful glaze for game and poultry or a bittersweet glaze for a dense chocolate cake. Or you can use just as you would plain orange marmalade.

Place kumquats, oranges, and water in glass bowl. Cover and let stand in a cool place for 12 hours. Pour into medium saucepan and bring to a full, rolling boil over high heat. Cook for about 15 minutes, stirring frequently. Remove from heat and stir in lemon and Grand Marnier. Measure this mixture and add equal amount of sugar. Again bring to a boil and cook, stirring frequently, for about 30 minutes. When mixture begins to gel, remove from heat and immediately pour into hot sterilized jars. Vacuum seal as directed on page 16.

GOURMET PRESERVES

Pumpkin Ginger Marmalade

This is sometimes called pumpkin pickle, sometimes pumpkin chip. I have experimented with the basic recipe and am delighted with its outcome.

QUANTITY:
6 ½-pint jars
PRESERVING METHOD USED:
Open kettle
STORAGE:
Vacuum-sealed—1 year
Refrigerated—6 weeks
May be frozen

Juice the 6 lemons. Put aside rinds. Place pumpkin chips, lemon juice, ginger, and sugar in glass bowl. Cover and let stand for 12 hours. Chop lemon rinds. Place in heavy saucepan and cover with water. Cook over medium heat for about 15 minutes. Drain and set aside. Over high heat, bring pumpkin mixture to a boil in heavy saucepan. Cook rapidly until pumpkin chips are translucent, about 45 minutes to 1 hour. Remove from heat. Remove pumpkin pieces from syrup and set aside. Bring syrup to a full, rolling boil and cook until slightly thickened. Add pumpkin and lemon rind. Bring to a boil and cook for 5 minutes. Immediately pour into hot sterilized jars and vacuum seal as directed on page 16.

6 *lemons, juice and rinds*
1 *small pumpkin, peeled, seeded, and sliced into thin ½-inch-square chips*
¼ *cup grated fresh ginger*
1 *cup sugar for each cup pumpkin*

Conserves, Marmalades, and Butters

65

Apple Brandy Butter

QUANTITY:
6 ½-pint jars
PRESERVING METHOD USED:
10-minute boiling water bath
STORAGE:
Vacuum-sealed—1 year
Refrigerated—2 months
May be frozen

6 cups fresh unsweetened,
  unspiced applesauce (see
  page 9)
½ cup Calvados
1 cup sugar
½ cup orange blossom honey
1 tablespoon ground cinnamon
¼ teaspoon ground cloves

The best! Use as a glaze, a spread, even whipped with sweet dairy butter for a breakfast or brunch treat. A special coating on wild game.

Place all ingredients in heavy saucepan. Bring to a boil over medium heat, stirring frequently. Cook for about 15 minutes, or until mixture begins to thicken. Pour into hot sterilized jars, leaving ¼-inch headspace. Cap and process in a 10-minute boiling water bath as directed on page 14.

Perfect Apple Butter

As pure as you can get. Just apples and a touch of cinnamon, if desired. Great for diets, both medical and caloric, since there is no sugar or salt. Use as a spread or as a dessert topping.

QUANTITY:
4 ½-pint jars
PRESERVING METHOD USED:
10-minute boiling water bath
STORAGE:
Vacuum-sealed—1 year
Refrigerated—3 weeks
May be frozen

Place apples and cider in heavy saucepan over medium heat. Cook, stirring frequently, until mixture comes to a boil. Lower heat and simmer, stirring frequently, for about 1 hour, or until apple slices have disintegrated and butter is thick. Remove from heat. Stir in cinnamon, if desired. Pour into hot sterilized jars, leaving ¼-inch headspace. Cap and process in a 10-minute boiling water bath as directed on page 14.

6 cups peeled and sliced sweet apples (such as McIntosh)
1 cup fresh apple cider
1 tablespoon ground cinnamon (optional)

Bourbon Butter

QUANTITY:
5 ½-pint jars
PRESERVING METHOD USED:
10-minute boiling water bath
STORAGE:
Vacuum-sealed—1 year
Refrigerated—6 weeks
May be frozen

5 cups fresh peach puree (see page 9)
1 cup good-quality bourbon
2 cups sugar
2 tablespoons chopped fresh mint

A fancy, rich butter that can be used as a coating on meats or game or as a spread for tea breads. It also makes a terrific filling for light cakes.

Place all ingredients in heavy saucepan over medium heat. Bring to a boil, stirring frequently. Lower heat and simmer for about 30 minutes, or until butter is thick. Remove from heat. Pour into hot sterilized jars, leaving ¼-inch headspace. Cap and process in a 10-minute boiling water bath as directed on page 14.

Ginger Pear Butter

The fresh ginger adds a bite to the richness of this fruit butter. A wonderful filling for crêpes with some chopped fresh pear added.

Place pears in heavy saucepan over medium heat. Add about ½ cup water. Cook, stirring frequently, until pears are soft. Add water if necessary, a little at a time, to prevent sticking. When pears are soft, remove from heat. Put pears in bowl of food processor and, using metal blade, process until smooth. Place pear puree in heavy saucepan. Add remaining ingredients. Bring to a boil over medium heat. Lower heat and cook, stirring frequently, for about 30 minutes, or until butter is thick. Remove from heat and immediately pour into hot sterilized jars, leaving ¼-inch headspace. Cap and process in a 10-minute boiling water bath as directed on page 14.

QUANTITY:
4 ½-pint jars
PRESERVING METHOD USED:
10-minute boiling water bath
STORAGE:
Vacuum-sealed—1 year
Refrigerated—4 weeks
May be frozen

8 cups cored and sliced pears
4 cups sugar
½ cup grated fresh ginger
1 teaspoon grated fresh lime rind
½ cup fresh lime juice
½ teaspoon chopped fresh sage

4

Spiced Fruits and Chutneys

Spiced fruits are whole fruits or, less frequently, uniform slices or pieces of fruit (either one type or mixed) that are cooked in a sweet, spicy syrup until plump. The fruit retains its shape but takes on some of the color of the spice. Also known as pickled fruits, they are usually served as an accompaniment to meat, poultry, or game. Spiced fruits may also be successfully used as dessert.

Chutneys are a hot, spicy-sweet mixed chopped fruit or vegetable jam-pickle. They can be exceedingly spicy, but the degree may be adjusted to individual taste. Authentically served with Indian curries, chutneys are also compatible with meats, poultry, and fish.

Spiced fruits require a 10-minute water bath for completion of the preserving process. Follow directions as described on page 14.

Chutneys are made by the open-kettle method and are vacuum-sealed either in canning jars with rubber-edged lids and caps or with hot, melted paraffin as described on page 16.

Both may be refrigerated for short-term storage as well as frozen for a period of no longer than 12 months.

Spiced Fruits and Chutneys

Peaches in Port Wine

Peaches in wine are a wonderful multipurpose preserve. Excellent as a condiment with roasted meats and super as a cold dessert served with delicate lace or butter cookies.

QUANTITY:
4 pint jars
PRESERVING METHOD USED:
10-minute boiling water bath
STORAGE:
Vacuum-sealed—1 year
Refrigerated—4 weeks

Combine peaches with all other ingredients in large nonaluminum saucepan over medium heat. Bring to a boil. Lower heat and simmer for 10 minutes. Remove from heat. Immediately pack 5 peaches into each hot sterilized jar, covering with syrup to ¼-inch headspace. Make sure that each jar has some peppercorns, cloves, and a cinnamon stick. Cap and process in a 10-minute boiling water bath as directed on page 14.

20 medium peaches, peeled
2½ cups sugar
3 cups water
3 cups port
2 tablespoons fresh lemon juice
Peel of 1 lemon, preferably in one long strip
Peel of 1 orange, preferably in one long strip
1 tablespoon whole white peppercorns
4 4-inch cinnamon sticks
12 whole cloves

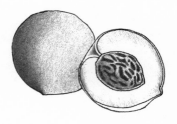

Moroccan Oranges

QUANTITY:
4 1/2-pint jars
PRESERVING METHOD USED:
5-minute boiling water bath
STORAGE:
Vacuum-sealed—1 year
Refrigerated—1 week

8 medium navel oranges,
  peeled and sliced
2 cups fresh orange juice
1/4 cup orange blossom water
1 teaspoon grated fresh lemon
  rind
1 teaspoon ground cinnamon
3 4-inch cinnamon sticks,
  broken into small pieces

These may be served cold as a dessert, with crisp greens as a salad, or in whipped cream as a cake filling. They may also be glazed with a bit of sweet butter under the broiler for use as a condiment or garnish for poultry or lamb.

Place all ingredients in heavy saucepan over medium heat. Bring to a boil. Remove from heat and immediately pack into hot sterilized jars, covering with syrup to 1/4-inch headspace. Cap and process in a 5-minute boiling water bath as directed on page 14.

Spiced Cranberry Cassis

This brings out the best in all poultry dishes—from roasts to cold salads. Over bittersweet chocolate ice cream, these cranberries make a sparkling dessert, especially if the sugar crystallizes, as it often does.

Place all ingredients in medium saucepan over high heat. Bring to a boil and cook for 7 minutes. Remove from heat and immediately pack into hot sterilized jars, making sure that each jar contains pieces of cinnamon stick, cloves, and 1 star anise. Vacuum seal as directed on page 16.

QUANTITY:
5 ½-pint jars
PRESERVING METHOD USED:
Open kettle
STORAGE:
Vacuum-sealed—1 year
Refrigerated—6 weeks

4 cups fresh cranberries, washed and dried
½ cup cider vinegar
¼ cup cassis
¼ cup water
2½ cups sugar
2 4-inch cinnamon sticks, broken into pieces
1 tablespoon whole cloves
5 whole star anise

Ginger Pears

QUANTITY:
4 pint jars
PRESERVING METHOD USED:
10-minute boiling water bath
STORAGE:
Vacuum-sealed—1 year
Refrigerated—6 weeks

These tiny whole pears make a superb dessert covered with ginger cream, as well as a garnish for roasted meats, poultry, and game. They are particularly good with roast goose.

Place water and lemon juice in large bowl. Peel pears, leaving on stems. As each is peeled, put into water-lemon bath. This will prevent pears from turning brown. Tie ginger, spices, and lemon into a cheesecloth bag. Place wine, water, juice, vinegar, and sugar in heavy saucepan. Add cheesecloth bag. Bring to a boil over medium heat. Lower

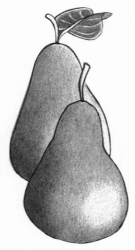

heat and cook for 10 minutes. Drain and dry a few pears at a time. Add to simmering syrup. (Do not pack pears into saucepan, as it will take them too long to cook, and they are more likely to be damaged.) Cook for about 10 minutes. Carefully remove pears and set them aside in heat-proof container with lid. Continue until all pears are cooked. Cover cooked pears with hot syrup. Cover and let stand in a cool place for about 12 hours. Bring pears and syrup to a boil, remove from heat, and immediately pack pears into hot sterilized jars, covering with boiling syrup to 1/4-inch headspace. Cap and process in a 10-minute boiling water bath as directed on page 14.

4 cups water
2 tablespoons fresh lemon juice
3 to 4 pounds firm Seckel pears with stems
1 cup peeled and sliced fresh ginger
1/2 cup stick cinnamon, broken into pieces
1/4 cup whole cloves
1 lemon, thinly sliced
2 cups dry white wine
1/2 cup water
1/2 cup apple juice
1 cup white vinegar
3 cups sugar

Marrons Glacés

QUANTITY:
6 pint jars
PRESERVING METHOD USED:
Open kettle
STORAGE:
Vacuum-sealed—1 year
Refrigerated—6 weeks

5 pounds whole raw chestnuts
5 cups sugar
2 cups water
1 cup dry white wine
2 whole cinnamon sticks
  (about 4 inches long)
1 2-inch piece vanilla bean
1 teaspoon ground cinnamon
1 teaspoon pure vanilla extract
½ cup good-quality brandy

* NOTE: If you use dried or processed nuts, you eliminate this section. Do not, however, use salted nuts.

This elegant French preserve has found its way into the American kitchen. I have also preserved other native nuts in this manner—pecans, black walnuts, English walnuts, and hazelnuts—for a delicious dessert.

Place nuts in large heavy saucepan. Cover with water and bring to a boil over high heat. Lower heat and cook for 30 minutes. Drain, cool, and peel chestnuts. * Set aside. Combine all other ingredients except brandy in heavy saucepan. Bring to a boil over medium heat. Boil for 5 minutes. Add peeled chestnuts and again bring to a boil. Lower heat and cook gently for about 30 minutes, or until chestnuts are transparent. Remove from heat and let stand in a cool place for 12 hours. Again bring to a boil. Cook for 10 minutes. Add brandy and again bring to a boil. Immediately remove from heat and pour into hot sterilized jars. Vacuum seal as directed on page 16.

GOURMET PRESERVES

Spiced Cherries

An old American favorite. My mom and aunts always had these on hand. They are an interesting garnish for meat and can also be used as a relish, like olives.

Place washed and dried cherries in glass bowl or crock with lid. Cover with apple cider vinegar, put cover on bowl, and let stand in a cool, dark place for 3 days. Drain off vinegar. Measure cherries. Add equal amount of sugar. Stir in ground spices. Cover and let stand in a cool, dark place for 3 more days. Turn cherries over once each day. Pour into hot sterilized jars and add a stick of cinnamon to each. Cover tightly and store in a cool, dark place or refrigerator for at least 4 weeks before use.

QUANTITY:
4 ½-pint jars
PRESERVING METHOD USED:
No processing required
STORAGE:
In a cool place, covered—up to 1 year

6 cups firm, ripe whole cherries, either sour or Bing (I prefer sour)
Apple cider vinegar
Sugar to equal fruit
4 tablespoons ground cinnamon
½ teaspoon ground cloves
4 2-inch cinnamon sticks

Lemon Chutney

QUANTITY:
4 ½-pint jars
PRESERVING METHOD USED:
Open kettle
STORAGE:
Vacuum-sealed—1 year
Refrigerated—2 months
May be frozen

2 cups cored and chopped
Granny Smith apples
1 cup chopped, mixed dried
fruit (no dates)
1½ cups seeded and chopped
whole lemon
½ cup chopped onions
1 clove garlic, minced
1 teaspoon whole mustard
seeds
1 cup white raisins
1 cup light brown sugar
½ cup white sugar
1 cup dry white wine
1 cup toasted pine nuts (or
almonds)
¼ cup anisette (or any other
anise-flavored liqueur)

This is my favorite chutney. Tart but sweet, an interesting side dish with lamb.

Place all ingredients, except pine nuts and anisette, in a heavy saucepan over medium heat. Cook for 30 minutes, stirring frequently. Do not boil. Remove from heat. Stir in toasted pine nuts and anisette. Immediately pour into hot sterilized jars. Vacuum seal as directed on page 16.

Tomato Chutney

An updated version of an old favorite. A bit spicy for some, but you can adjust to your taste by lessening the hot pepper measurement. I usually make it even hotter for my family's taste.

Combine all ingredients in heavy saucepan over medium heat. Cook, stirring frequently, for 2 hours, or until mixture is quite thick. Immediately pour into hot sterilized jars and vacuum seal as directed on page 16.

QUANTITY:
8 ½-pint jars
PRESERVING METHOD USED:
Open kettle
STORAGE:
Vacuum-sealed—1 year
Refrigerated—3 months
May be frozen

4 cups peeled, cored, and chopped red tomatoes
4 cups cored and chopped green tomatoes
4 cups peeled, cored, and chopped Granny Smith apples
2 cups chopped red onions
½ cup seeded and chopped red and green peppers
3 jalapeño peppers, seeded and chopped
¼ cup chopped fresh coriander
2 tablespoons grated fresh ginger
3 large cloves garlic, peeled and mashed
1 cup seedless black raisins
3 cups light brown sugar
3 cups apple cider vinegar
1 teaspoon cayenne pepper
1 teaspoon ground cinnamon
Salt to taste

Onion Chutney

QUANTITY:
4 ½-pint jars
PRESERVING METHOD USED:
Open kettle
STORAGE:
Vacuum-sealed—1 year
Refrigerated—6 weeks
May be frozen

6 cups chopped Vidalia onions
   (other sweet onions may
   also be used)
½ cup fresh lemon juice
2 teaspoons whole cumin seed
1 teaspoon whole mustard seed
½ teaspoon Tabasco sauce
¼ teaspoon red pepper flakes
2 teaspoons ground chili pepper
¼ cup light brown sugar
Salt to taste

Easy to make, easier to eat. A spicy onion garnish for meats or sandwiches.

Combine all ingredients in heavy saucepan over medium heat. Bring to a boil, stirring frequently. When mixture comes to a boil, immediately remove from heat and pack into hot sterilized jars. Vacuum seal as directed on page 16.

Rhubarb Chutney

A Victorian favorite updated by the use of red wine. Excellent with roasts.

Combine all ingredients in heavy saucepan over medium heat. Bring to a boil, stirring frequently. Lower heat and cook for about 30 minutes, or until mixture is thick. Immediately pour into hot sterilized jars. Vacuum seal as directed on page 16.

QUANTITY:
6 ½-pint jars
PRESERVING METHOD USED:
Open kettle
STORAGE:
Vacuum-sealed—1 year
Refrigerated—6 weeks
May be frozen

6 cups chopped rhubarb
1 cup chopped red onions
3 cloves garlic, peeled and minced
½ cup peeled and chopped celery
1 large green apple, peeled, cored, and chopped
1 cup dried currants
2½ cups light brown sugar
¾ cup dry red wine
1 teaspoon grated fresh ginger
1 teaspoon ground cinnamon
¼ teaspoon ground cloves

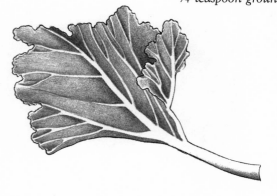

Celery Apple Chutney

QUANTITY:
6 ½-pint jars
PRESERVING METHOD USED:
Open kettle
STORAGE:
Vacuum-sealed—1 year
Refrigerated—6 weeks

6 cups peeled, cored, and
    chopped green apples
1 medium red pepper, seeded
    and chopped
½ cup chopped onions
3 cloves garlic, peeled and
    minced
1 cup white raisins
¼ cup chopped candied ginger
1 cup light brown sugar
3 tablespoons whole mustard
    seed
½ cup white wine vinegar
1½ cups finely chopped celery

Crunchier than other chutneys, and with a lovely mustard flavor. A terrific base for dressings used on mixed vegetables or meat or poultry salads.

Place all ingredients, except celery, in heavy saucepan over medium heat. Bring to a boil. Lower heat, cover, and cook, stirring occasionally, for about 25 minutes, or until mixture begins to thicken. Immediately add celery and cook for an additional 5 minutes. Remove from heat and pour into hot sterilized jars. Vacuum seal as directed on page 16.

What I Think Is Traditional Chutney

This is the closest I've been able to come to the tasty Major Grey's Chutney that is traditionally served with Indian curries. Although the original recipe is secret and, to my knowledge, never printed, I have used the same ingredients as those listed on the bottle.

Place all ingredients in heavy saucepan over medium heat. Bring to a boil. Lower heat and simmer for about 20 minutes, stirring frequently. Remove from heat, cover, and let stand for about 12 hours. Again bring to a boil, lower heat, and cook for 15 minutes, stirring frequently. Remove from heat and immediately pour into hot sterilized jars. Vacuum seal as directed on page 16.

QUANTITY:
4 ½-pint jars
PRESERVING METHOD USED:
Open kettle
STORAGE:
Vacuum-sealed—1 year
Refrigerated—6 weeks
May be frozen

4 cups peeled, seeded, and sliced hard, ripe mango
½ cup seeded and chopped lime
1 cup chopped yellow onions
½ cup grated fresh ginger
3 cloves garlic, peeled and minced
¾ cup white raisins
2 cups light brown sugar
1 cup apple cider vinegar
¼ cup fresh orange juice
¼ cup fresh lemon juice
1 tablespoon whole mustard seed
1 teaspoon dried red pepper flakes
1 teaspoon ground cinnamon
¼ teaspoon ground cloves

5

Relishes and Pickles

Relishes are made of vegetables or fruits or a combination of vegetables and fruits. The vegetables and fruits used are finely sliced, shredded, or chopped. Made with vinegar and spices and/or herbs, relishes may be either sweet or sour, spicy or plain. Only recently rediscovered, they are used as an accompaniment to meat, poultry, or game and as a dressing on sandwiches or salads.

Pickles are also made of vegetables or fruits. They may be left whole, sliced, chopped, or peeled according to the type of pickle desired. Vegetables may be pickled by the use of salt or vinegar, or by vinegar and salt in combination. Fruits are pickled by the use of vinegar, sugar, and spices. Whole spices should be tied in a thin cloth bag, unless otherwise directed. Some pickles are crunchy and crisp to the taste, while others are firm but have lost their crispness through cooking.

For all crisp pickles, I recommend the use of kosher salt and white distilled vinegar. Slightly underripe vegetables or fruits will also be crunchier to the taste.

Pickles are made by both the open-kettle and water bath method as required by the individual recipe. If using the water bath method, the processing time required will be given with the individual recipe. If using the open-kettle method, vacuum seal in canning jars for pickles, or for relishes you may use hot, melted paraffin as directed on page 16.

Both may be refrigerated for short-term storage. Relishes may be frozen for a period of no longer than 12 months. *Vegetable pickles may not be frozen.*

Relishes and Pickles

RELISHES
Mom's Pepper Relish • Faye's Zucchini Relish • Spiced Cranberry Relish • Pennsylvania Corn Relish • Fresh Beet Relish • Fruit Relish • Summer Relish

PICKLES
Pickled Okra • Sichuan Pickles • Pickled Peppers • Pickled Baby Vegetables • Vidalia Onion Pickle • Tex-Mex Pickle • Sour Onion Pickle

Mom's Pepper Relish

My husband's very favorite. He uses it on sandwiches, salads, meats, poultry, and sometimes he just eats it plain. Most endearing to a mother-in-law!

Using shredding blade of food processor, finely shred peppers and onions. Place in bowl and cover with boiling water. Let stand for 5 minutes. Drain well. Place pepper mixture, 2 cups vinegar, and 2 cups water in heavy saucepan over medium heat. Bring to a boil. Remove from heat. Let stand for 10 minutes, then drain thoroughly. Add 2 cups vinegar, sugar, and salt. Again bring to a boil. Lower heat and cook, stirring occasionally, for about 30 minutes. When mixture has thickened, remove from heat and immediately pour into hot sterilized jars. Vacuum seal as directed on page 16.

QUANTITY:
8 pint jars
PRESERVING METHOD USED:
Open kettle
STORAGE:
Vacuum-sealed—1 year
Refrigerated—6 weeks
May be frozen

9 *sweet red peppers, seeded and sliced*
9 *sweet green peppers, seeded and sliced*
3 *jalapeño or serrano peppers (optional)*
9 *onions, quartered*
Boiling water
4 *cups vinegar*
2 *cups water*
3 *cups sugar*
1 *teaspoon salt*

Faye's Zucchini Relish

QUANTITY:
8 ½-pint jars
PRESERVING METHOD USED:
Open kettle
STORAGE:
Vacuum-sealed—1 year
Refrigerated—6 weeks
May be frozen

A friend's mother's answer to the bounty of the summer garden. I truly believe that all zucchini recipes have been developed because of the plant's ability to grow and grow and grow. In the summer, there seems to appear a zucchini fairy who leaves, at my back door, 2 or 3 unasked for bushels of zucchini. It also seems to appear at the doors of friends, so I know it exists! This is so tasty you will wish it would multiply on your shelf. May be used on sandwiches, cold meats, and fish, or in salads.

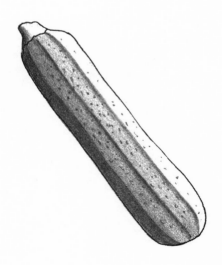

Place grated vegetables in nonaluminum bowl. Sprinkle on salt. Mix well, cover, and let stand for 12 hours. Rinse well by running cold water over vegetable mixture in colander. Drain thoroughly. Place vinegar, sugar, and spices in heavy saucepan over medium heat. Bring to a boil. Lower heat and cook for about 15 minutes, or until mixture begins to thicken. Immediately add vegetable mixture and cook for 30 minutes. Remove from heat. Pour into hot sterilized jars. Vacuum seal as directed on page 16.

6 *cups grated zucchini*
3 *cups grated yellow onions*
1 *sweet red pepper, seeded and grated*
1 *sweet green pepper, seeded and grated*
3 *tablespoons coarse salt*
1¼ *cups white vinegar*
3 *cups sugar*
½ *teaspoon dry mustard*
½ *teaspoon ground nutmeg*
½ *teaspoon ground tumeric*
1 *teaspoon celery seed*
½ *teaspoon fresh ground black pepper*

NOTE: You may grate all vegetables in the food processor using the shredder blade.

Spiced Cranberry Relish

QUANTITY:
4 ½-pint jars
PRESERVING METHOD USED:
Open kettle
STORAGE:
Vacuum-sealed—1 year
Refrigerated—6 weeks
May be frozen

4½ cups fresh cranberries
¼ cup grated fresh orange rind
¼ cup grated fresh lemon rind
1 tablespoon minced fresh
    jalpeño pepper
¼ teaspoon dried red pepper
    flakes
1 cup raw honey
⅔ cup red wine vinegar
1 tablespoon mustard seed
¼ teaspoon ground ginger
Salt to taste

A variation on the traditional Thanksgiving cranberry relish. Also may be used as an accompaniment to pâtés and other terrines.

Place all ingredients in heavy saucepan over medium heat. Bring to a boil. Lower heat and simmer for 15 minutes. Remove from heat and immediately pour into hot sterilized jars. Vacuum seal as directed on page 16.

Pennsylvania Corn Relish

Throughout the Amish communities corn relish is always on the table. However, it is almost never seen outside rural communities anymore—perhaps because of the scarcity of fresh, sweet corn. Although it is generally used as a condiment or accompaniment, I combine a jar with 4 cups cold rice or pasta, add a little homemade mayonnaise, and have a lovely summer salad. Add some cold leftover meat or poultry, and you have a nice main course meal.

Place all ingredients in heavy saucepan over medium heat. Bring to a boil. Lower heat and simmer gently for 20 minutes. Remove from heat. Immediately pour into hot sterilized jars. Vacuum seal as directed on page 16.

QUANTITY:
8 ½-pint jars
PRESERVING METHOD USED:
Open kettle
STORAGE:
Vacuum-sealed—1 year
Refrigerated—8 weeks

6 cups cut fresh corn
2 cups finely shredded green cabbage
2 cups chopped yellow onions
1 cup seeded and diced sweet red pepper
2 teaspoons whole celery seed
1 teaspoon whole mustard seed
1 teaspoon ground tumeric
1 teaspoon dry mustard
¾ cup sugar
1 cup cider vinegar

Fresh Beet Relish

QUANTITY:
4 ½-pint jars
PRESERVING METHOD USED:
Open kettle
STORAGE:
Vacuum-sealed—1 year
Refrigerated—6 weeks

6 cups peeled and shredded
  raw beets
1 cup grated fresh horseradish
1 cup grated red onions
1 cup grated zucchini
1½ cups sugar
2 cups distilled vinegar
1 teaspoon dried red pepper
  flakes (optional)

This is a perfect mate for boiled dinners. It is also a superb base for salad dressings.

Place all ingredients in heavy saucepan over medium heat. Bring to a boil. Lower heat and simmer for 20 minutes. Remove from heat and immediately pour into hot sterilized jars. Vacuum seal as directed on page 16.

Fruit Relish

This is a great relish to make in August when peaches, pears, and tomatoes are ready for harvest. It is good on meats or with brunch dishes.

Place all ingredients in heavy saucepan over medium heat. Bring to a boil. Lower heat and cook for 1 hour, stirring frequently to prevent scorching. Remove from heat. Immediately pour into hot sterilized jars. Vacuum seal as directed on page 16.

QUANTITY:
6 ½-pint jars
PRESERVING METHOD USED:
Open kettle
STORAGE:
Vacuum-sealed—1 year
Refrigerated—6 weeks
May be frozen

2 cups peeled and chopped ripe tomatoes
2 cups peeled and shredded pears
2 cups peeled and chopped peaches
1 cup seeded and grated red sweet peppers
1 cup grated onions
¼ cup peeled and grated fresh ginger
1½ cups cider vinegar
½ cup fruit brandy
2 cups light brown sugar
1 teaspoon celery seed
1 teaspoon dry mustard
1 teaspoon ground cinnamon

Summer Relish

QUANTITY:
6 1/2-pint jars
PRESERVING METHOD USED:
No processing required
STORAGE:
Refrigerated, covered—3
  months

3 cups peeled and chopped ripe
  tomatoes
1 cup peeled and chopped
  green tomatoes
1 cup chopped onions
1 cup finely shredded cabbage
1 sweet green pepper, seeded
  and chopped
1/2 cup peeled and grated sweet
  apple
2 teaspoons prepared grated
  horseradish
2 tablespoons mustard seed
1/3 cup light brown sugar
1 teaspoon Tabasco sauce
1 1/2 cups cider vinegar

This needs no cooking, so it is a perfect preserve to do on a hot summer day when vegetables are at their best. A great relish for grilled meats and for salad dressings.

Mix all ingredients together in glass bowl. Cover and refrigerate for 24 hours before eating. If relish gets too juicy, drain off some of the liquid. Cover and refrigerate for up to 3 months.

Pickled Okra

The interest in Cajun cooking has led to the nationwide discovery of okra, a vegetable that has been most frequently associated with the South. Made into pickle, it is crisp and delicious, and is a particularly wonderful hors d'oeuvre.

Place vinegar, water, and salt in heavy saucepan over medium heat. Bring to a boil and cook for 5 minutes. In the meantime pack each sterilized jar with about 10 okra pods, 1 garlic clove, 1 hot pepper, and 1 teaspoon each of dill and mustard seed. Pour boiling liquid into each jar, leaving ½-inch headspace. Cap and process in a 5-minute boiling water bath as directed on page 14.

QUANTITY:
6 ½-pint jars
PRESERVING METHOD USED:
5-minute boiling water bath
STORAGE:
Vacuum-sealed—1 year
Refrigerated—3 months

2 cups cider vinegar
1 cup water
¼ cup kosher salt
60 young, tender okra pods, washed and dried (about 4 pounds)
6 cloves garlic, peeled
6 jalapeño or serrano peppers
6 teaspoons dill seed
6 teaspoons mustard seed

Sichuan Pickles

QUANTITY:
6 ½-pint jars
PRESERVING METHOD USED:
10-minute boiling water bath
STORAGE:
Vacuum-sealed—1 year
Refrigerated—6 weeks

3 tablespoons soy sauce
¾ cup red wine vinegar
¾ cup light brown sugar
8 large cucumbers, peeled,
seeded, and cut into ½-inch
slices
¼ cup coarse salt
½ cup peanut oil
2 tablespoons Sichuan
peppercorns
1 tablespoon dried red pepper
flakes
½ cup shredded and soaked
Chinese mushrooms
¼ cup grated fresh ginger
2 cloves garlic, peeled and
minced
6 whole red chipotle chilies

Almost every town in America seems to have a Chinese restaurant, and every gourmet kitchen has a wok. This pickle is a great accompaniment to not only Sichuan cuisine but to any Chinese food. It can also add zest to any American meal.

Mix soy sauce, vinegar, and sugar together in glass bowl. Cover and set aside for at least 1 hour. Cut cucumbers into very thin slices. Place in another glass bowl. Stir in salt. Cover and let stand for 1 hour. Pour oil and peppercorns into wok. Heat to smoking. Lower heat and cook until peppercorns are black. Remove from heat. Cover. Let stand for 20 minutes. Remove peppercorns. Add all other ingredients except cucumber slices, and bring to a boil, stirring frequently. Drain cucumbers, squeezing out as much liquid as possible. Stir into hot liquid. Pack into hot sterilized jars, leaving ½-inch headspace. Cap and process in a 10-minute boiling water bath as directed on page 14.

Sour Onion Pickle

Perfect as a pop-in-your-mouth cocktail tidbit. Great in salads and sandwiches or as a garnish for cold meats.

Place peeled onions in glass or ceramic bowl. Sprinkle in salt and add cold water to cover. Let stand in a cool place for 12 hours. Drain off salt water and rinse in colander under cold running water. Drain and dry. Bring all other ingredients to a boil in heavy saucepan over medium heat. Lower heat and simmer for 15 minutes. In the meantime pack onions into hot sterilized jars. Pour pickling syrup over onions, leaving ¼-inch headspace. Make sure that each jar contains a red pepper. Cap and process in a 10-minute boiling water bath as directed on page 14.

QUANTITY:
4 ½-pint jars
PRESERVING METHOD USED:
10-minute boiling water bath
STORAGE:
Vacuum-sealed—1 year
Refrigerated—2 months

4 cups pearl onions (the very smallest you can find)
¼ cup salt
3 cups white vinegar
1 tablespoon fresh orange juice
¼ cup sugar
1 tablespoon mustard seed
1 tablespoon grated fresh horseradish
4 dried hot red chili peppers

Pickled Peppers

QUANTITY:
6 pint jars
PRESERVING METHOD USED:
10-minute boiling water bath
STORAGE:
Vacuum-sealed—1 year
Refrigerated—3 months

This sensational pickle is as sophisticated as one can imagine, yet it comes from the North Union Shaker settlement of the mid-1800s. It was always in great demand by the outside world, and is still addictive. Can be used as an appetizer as well as a garnish or accompaniment.

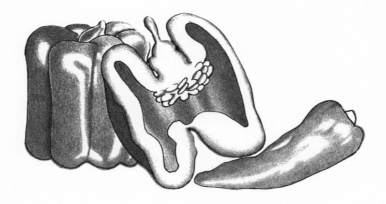

Neatly cut tops off peppers. Seed, being careful not to break peppers. Place peppers and tops, salt, and 1 gallon water in large glass or ceramic bowl. Cover and let stand for 24 hours. Drain. Rinse in colander under running cold water until free of brine. Drain and dry. Set aside.

Place vinegar, 2 cups water, and sugar in heavy saucepan over medium heat. Bring to a boil. Lower heat and let simmer while stuffing peppers. Mix all remaining ingredients together and stuff into peppers. Replace tops on peppers. Hold tops in place with toothpicks, or sew with needle and heavy thread. Pack peppers into hot sterilized jars, about 3 per jar. Pour hot pickling syrup over peppers, leaving ¼-inch headspace. Cap and process in a 10-minute boiling water bath as directed on page 14.

18 small to medium whole green and/or red sweet peppers (you may also use green tomatoes or a mixture of peppers and green tomatoes)
1 cup coarse salt
1 gallon water
4 cups distilled white vinegar
2 cups water
½ cup sugar
1 small head green cabbage, finely shredded
1 cup grated fresh horseradish
3 cups finely shredded onions
⅓ cup mustard seed
1 teaspoon ground pepper
3 teaspoons ground cloves
Salt to taste

Vidalia Onion Pickle

QUANTITY:
6 pint jars
PRESERVING METHOD USED:
10-minute boiling water bath
STORAGE:
Vacuum-sealed—1 year
Refrigerated—6 weeks

6 pounds Vidalia onions,
    quartered
1/4 cup salt
Ice chips
5 cups sugar
5 cups distilled vinegar
2 teaspoons celery seed
1 teaspoon dry mustard
2 teaspoons ground tumeric

The Vidalia onion is grown in small quantities in rural Georgia. Renowned for their sweetness and desired for their rarity, these native American onions make a superb pickle to be used chopped in a sandwich filling or as a condiment, relish, or hors d'oeuvre on a water biscuit with cream cheese.

Layer onions, salt, and ice chips in 3 layers in glass or ceramic bowl. Cover and let stand for 3 hours. Drain in colander. Do not rinse. Squeeze with paper towels to remove extra liquid. Set aside. Bring all other ingredients to a hard boil in heavy saucepan over medium heat. Add onions and again bring to a boil. Cook for 3 minutes. Pour into hot sterilized jars, leaving 1/2-inch headspace. Cap and process in a 10-minute boiling water bath as directed on page 14.

Tex-Mex Pickle

You can use this as a salad mixed with lettuce, as a garnish for any filled tortilla entree, or just as a fresh spicy pickle.

Toss all vegetables together with salt. Let stand for 1 hour. Rinse thoroughly, drain, and dry. Place all other ingredients in heavy saucepan over medium heat. Bring to a boil. Lower heat and cook for 10 minutes. In the meantime pack vegetables into hot sterilized jars. Pour boiling pickling syrup into each jar, leaving ¼-inch headspace. Cap and process in a 5-minute boiling water bath as directed on page 14.

QUANTITY:
6 ½-pint jars
PRESERVING METHOD USED:
5-minute boiling water bath
STORAGE:
Vacuum-sealed—1 year
Refrigerated—6 weeks

2 large jícamas, peeled and
   sliced into thin strips
1 large sweet red pepper, cored
   and cut into strips
1 cup sliced onions
½ cup chopped scallions
1 cup sliced and seeded
   Anaheim chilies
1 cup radishes, cut into
   quarters
¼ cup salt
3 cups white vinegar
½ cup fresh lime juice
½ cup water
2 cups sugar
¼ cup chopped fresh coriander

Pickled Baby Vegetables

QUANTITY:
4 ½-pint jars
PRESERVING METHOD USED:
10-minute boiling water bath
STORAGE:
Vacuum-sealed—1 year
Refrigerated—2 months

These are especially appealing as a cocktail tidbit or in a salade composé. Although this recipe calls for baby vegetables, you can make these with pieces or sticks of any mature vegetable.

Place vegetables in heavy saucepan. Add water and salt. Bring to a boil, cover, and let stand for 5 minutes (except sugar snap peas, which should be removed as soon as water comes to a boil). Drain, reserving 2 cups cooking liquid. Set vegetables aside. Add cooking liquid to remaining ingredients in heavy saucepan. Bring to a boil over medium heat. Boil hard for 10 minutes. Remove cinnamon stick. Pack vegetables into hot sterilized jars, leaving ½-inch headspace. Make sure each jar contains 1 chili, 1 sprig of dill, and 1 garlic clove with hot pickling syrup. Cap and process in a 10-minute boiling water bath as directed on page 14.

3 pounds mixed baby vegetables (for instance, carrots, green beans, corn, sugar snap peas, eggplant, or pattypan squash)
4 cups water
1 teaspoon salt
2 cups white wine vinegar
1 tablespoon pickling spice
1 tablespoon cracked black pepper
1 cinnamon stick
4 hot red chilies
4 sprigs fresh dill
4 cloves garlic, peeled

6

Condiments and Salad Dressings

Condiments are made of finely chopped and cooked vegetables and/or fruits. The foods used in preparing many condiments are cooked until tender and then pureed. Usually cooked with vinegars and highly seasoned with spices and peppers, condiments are thick, saucelike liquids served as sandwich dressing or as seasoning for meats, fish, poultry, game, and, occasionally, vegetables.

Salad dressings are made of a combination of oils, vinegars, and seasonings. Eggs, creams, and cheeses add variety to dressings that are used with vegetable, green, or pasta salads, while fruit juices, sweeteners, and creams complement the basic ingredients for use on fruits.

Condiments and salad dressings are preserved by cooking in an open kettle and vacuum sealing in canning jars with rubber-edged lids and caps as directed on page 16.

If long storage is required, salad dressings are processed in a 10-minute boiling water bath as directed on page 14.

Both may be refrigerated for up to 6 weeks and frozen for a period of no more than 12 months, or as directed in the individual recipe.

Condiments and Salad Dressings

CONDIMENTS

*Spicy Beer Mustard • Bahamian Old Sour • "Nouvelle" Catsup •
Salsa Inferno • Condensed Onions • Blueberry Catsup • Red
Pepper Mustard • Fresh Horseradish • Mushroom Catsup • Basic
Tex-Mex Salsa*

SALAD DRESSINGS

*Hot and Sour Salad Dressing • Old-Fashioned Boiled Dressing •
Jalapeño Dressing • Vegetarian Dressing • Sesame Seed Dressing •
Fruit Salad Dressing*

Spicy Beer Mustard

Use this whenever you would normally use mustard. It's just better! It also makes a terrific coating on grilled meats or poultry.

Combine mustard seed, beer, and vinegar in glass bowl. Cover and let stand for 4 hours. Stir in remaining ingredients. Place in heavy saucepan over low heat. Cook, stirring constantly, for 10 minutes. Add beer, a drop or two at a time, if mixture seems too dry. Pour into hot sterilized jars. Cap and process in a 15-minute boiling water bath as directed on page 14.

QUANTITY:
4 ½-pint jars
PRESERVING METHOD USED:
15-minute boiling water bath
STORAGE:
Vacuum-sealed—1 year
Refrigerated—3 months
May be frozen

1 cup whole mustard seed
1 cup good beer or ale
¼ cup white wine vinegar
3 cups dry English mustard
¾ cup light brown sugar
1 teaspoon Tabasco sauce
Salt to taste

Bahamian Old Sour

QUANTITY:
4 ½-pint jars
PRESERVING METHOD USED:
No processing required
STORAGE:
*In a cool place, tightly
   covered—up to 1 year*

4 cups fresh Key lime, lime,
   lemon, or sour orange juice
2 tablespoons salt
16 bird peppers, red chili
   peppers, or any other hot
   pepper you prefer

We were introduced to this as a seasoning on conch in Harbour Island, the Bahamas. Every cook has a jar or two on the shelf. Every island roadside food stand has its own homemade Old Sour. We have become addicted to it. Perfect for sprinkling on fish, either before or after cooking, and on vegetables and salads.

Mix juice and salt. Stir until salt is dissolved. Pour into hot sterilized jars. Add 4 peppers per bottle. Screw clean caps on tightly and set aside to ferment for at least 10 days before use.

Salsa Inferno

This is the hottest sauce I know for garnishing Tex-Mex foods—tacos, burritos, and the like. It can also be used on grilled meats and vegetables, but remember, it is *hot!*

Place all ingredients in heavy saucepan over medium heat. Bring to a boil. Remove from heat and immediately pack into hot sterilized jars. Vacuum seal as directed on page 16.

QUANTITY:
3 ½-pint jars
PRESERVING METHOD USED:
Open kettle
STORAGE:
Vacuum-sealed—1 year
Refrigerated—4 weeks
May be frozen

4 cups peeled and chopped fresh tomatoes
1 cup chopped mild green chilies
½ cup minced onions
2 tablespoons minced fresh garlic
½ cup chopped scallions
½ cup chopped and seeded fresh jalapeño peppers
1 tablespoon Tabasco sauce
3 tablespoons distilled white vinegar
Salt, if desired

"Nouvelle" Catsup

QUANTITY:
4 ½-pint jars
PRESERVING METHOD USED:
20-minute boiling water bath
STORAGE:
Vacuum-sealed—1 year
Refrigerated—1 week
May be frozen

Not really a catsup, but it is used as a sauce or accompaniment to game (venison in particular) or meat, especially pork. Using no salt, no oil, and no cream, this is most useful when you're on a diet.

Place all vegetables and fruits on steaming rack in heavy saucepan, laying lemon peel and ginger pieces on top. Pour enough water into bottom of pan to keep an active steam going in which to cook vegetables. This is the best method for holding their flavor. If you do not have a steamer, you can cook vegetables and fruits directly in heavy saucepan with just enough water to cover. Layer lemon peel and ginger pieces

112

on top. When fruits and vegetables are soft, remove from heat. Discard lemon peel and ginger. Drain fruits and vegetables, reserving cooking liquid.

Using either food processor, blender, or food mill, puree fruits and vegetables. Add lemon juice. If more liquid is required, use cooking liquid to make a smooth puree. When all vegetables and fruits are pureed, place in heavy saucepan over medium heat. Stir in Tabasco and pepper to taste. Add salt, if desired. Simmer for about 5 minutes. Immediately pour into hot sterilized jars, leaving ½-inch headspace. Cap and process in a 20-minute boiling water bath as directed on page 14.

4 cups peeled and sliced white turnips
3 cups peeled, cored, and chopped tart apples
1 cup peeled and sliced parsnips
1 cup peeled, cored, and sliced ripe pears
2 stalks celery, peeled and cubed
1 4-inch lemon peel
1 1-inch fresh ginger, peeled and quartered
1 tablespoon fresh lemon juice
Dash Tabasco sauce
Fresh ground pepper to taste
Salt to taste, if desired

Condensed Onions

QUANTITY:
3 ½-pint jars
PRESERVING METHOD USED:
Open kettle
STORAGE:
Vacuum-sealed—1 year
Refrigerated—2 months

¾ cup sweet butter
2 tablespoons virgin olive oil
8 cups halved and sliced sweet
onions
2 cloves garlic, peeled and
minced
½ cup superfine sugar
½ cup fruit vinegar
1 teaspoon minced fresh thyme

A special condiment for game or poultry. The sweeter the onion (Vidalia or Walla-Walla onions are best), the richer the preserve.

Melt butter with oil in heavy saucepan over low heat. Stir in onions and garlic. Cook for about 10 minutes. Add sugar, vinegar, and thyme. Cook, stirring constantly, until sugar is dissolved and mixture begins to turn caramel colored. If, during cooking, more liquid is needed to keep onions from scorching, add additional fruit vinegar. When mixture is thick, pour into hot sterilized jars. Vacuum seal as directed on page 16.

Blueberry Catsup

Another hand-me-down from the North Union Shaker settlement, and one of my favorite condiments for "nouvelle American" cuisine.

Place all ingredients in heavy saucepan over medium heat. Bring to a boil. Lower heat and simmer, stirring frequently, until berries are pureed and catsup is thick. Immediately pour into hot sterilized jars. Vacuum seal as directed on page 16.

QUANTITY:
4 1/2-pint jars
PRESERVING METHOD USED:
Open kettle
STORAGE:
Vacuum-sealed—1 year
Refrigerated—1 year
May be frozen

5 cups fresh blueberries
3 cups sugar
1 tablespoon fresh lemon juice
1 tablespoon ground cinnamon
2 teaspoons ground cloves
1 teaspoon fresh ground black pepper
1/2 teaspoon salt (or to taste)
3/4 cup blueberry vinegar

Red Pepper Mustard

QUANTITY:
4 ½-pint jars
PRESERVING METHOD USED:
Open kettle
STORAGE:
Vacuum-sealed—1 year
Refrigerated—3 months
May be frozen

1 cup fine dry English mustard
¼ cup light brown sugar
½ teaspoon Tabasco
1 cup fruit vinegar
1 cup water
4 cups cooked sweet red
  pepper puree
½ cup dry sherry
¼ cup mustard seed
¼ teaspoon ground oregano
¾ cup cooked and chopped red
  and green sweet peppers

A perfect mustard for all types of sandwiches, as well as a special coating for roast pork or lamb. Mix with whipped cream or cook a bit with heavy cream and you will have an "haute cuisine" sauce.

In glass bowl mix together dry mustard, sugar, Tabasco, vinegar, and water. Cover and let stand for 3 hours. In heavy saucepan over medium heat bring red pepper puree, sherry, mustard seed, and oregano to a boil. Add mustard mixture and again bring to a boil. Lower heat and cook, stirring constantly, until mixture is fairly thick. Quickly stir in cooked pepper pieces and immediately pour into hot sterilized jars. Vacuum seal as directed on page 16.

116

Fresh Horseradish

I first discovered the ease of preparation and fresh taste of home-canned horseradish in the Pennsylvania Amish country. I use it so frequently in sauces, salads, and on sandwiches, and particularly as a low-calorie relish, that I always like to have it on hand.

Pack grated horseradish (and beet, if desired) into hot sterilized jars. Fill to the top with vinegar. Cover with a tight seal and store in a cool, dark place. Allow to mellow 1 week before using.

QUANTITY:
6 ½-pint jars
PRESERVING METHOD USED:
No processing required
STORAGE:
In a cool place, tightly
    sealed—up to 1 year

3 pounds fresh horseradish,
    peeled and grated fine
1 raw beet, grated fine, if
    desired (for red color and a
    bit of a different taste)
1½ cups excellent white
    vinegar or white herb
    vinegar

Mushroom Catsup

QUANTITY:
4 ½-pint jars
PRESERVING METHOD USED:
Open kettle
STORAGE:
Vacuum-sealed—1 year
Refrigerated—1 week
May be frozen

8 cups chopped fresh
  mushrooms
1 tablespoon salt
1 cup chopped onions
1 jalapeño pepper, seeded and
  chopped, if desired
2 cloves garlic, peeled and
  minced
1 teaspoon commercial pickling
  spices
1 tablespoon chopped fresh
  parsley
½ cup herb vinegar

An interesting variation of America's most used condiment. A long-forgotten recipe perfect for all grilled meats.

Place chopped mushrooms and salt in glass bowl. Stir to mix. Cover and set aside for 24 hours. Then place mushrooms and all other ingredients in heavy saucepan over medium heat. Bring to a boil. Lower heat and simmer for about 45 minutes. Remove from heat. Drain, reserving all liquid. Puree mushroom mixture in food processor, adding liquid as needed to make a thick catsuplike sauce. Place puree in heavy saucepan over medium heat. Bring to a boil. Immediately pour into hot sterilized jars. Vacuum seal as directed on page 16.

118

Basic Tex-Mex Salsa

Everyone seems to love the cooking of the American Southwest. Although this sauce is used on all manner of tortilla-filled entrées, it can just as appropriately be used as a condiment on any meat or vegetable. It also makes a tasty grilled-cheese sandwich. This sauce can be used raw.

If using raw or freezing, mix all vegetables together, cover, and let stand for about 30 minutes. Refrigerate or freeze as directed on page 15. To can salsa, place all ingredients in heavy saucepan over medium heat. Cook until just boiling. Immediately pour into hot sterilized jars and vacuum seal as directed on page 16.

QUANTITY:
4 ½-pint jars
PRESERVING METHOD USED:
Open kettle
STORAGE:
Vacuum-sealed—1 year
Refrigerated—6 weeks
May be frozen (if freezing, do not cook)

4 cups seeded and chopped ripe tomatoes
1 cup finely chopped red onions
2 cloves garlic, peeled and mashed
½ cup seeded and chopped mild green chilies
1 jalapeño pepper, seeded and minced
¼ cup chopped fresh cilantro
¼ cup red wine vinegar
2 tablespoons olive oil

NOTE: If you use a food processor, take care not to puree. This sauce should have a chunky texture.

Hot and Sour Salad Dressing

QUANTITY:
3 ½-pint jars
PRESERVING METHOD USED:
Open kettle
STORAGE:
Vacuum-sealed—1 year
Refrigerated—1 week
May be frozen

2½ cups vegetable bouillon (or
  fresh vegetable stock)
¼ cup soy sauce
½ cup fruit vinegar
¼ cup dry white wine
2 tablespoons hot chili oil
⅓ cup crunchy peanut butter
¼ cup pure vegetable oil
2 tablespoons sesame seeds
2 tablespoons grated fresh
  ginger
2 cloves garlic, peeled and
  minced
2 teaspoons dried red pepper
  flakes (or to taste)

This Chinese-inspired salad dressing is perfect for pasta, poultry, and vegetable or mixed green salads.

Place all ingredients in bowl of food processor. Using metal blade and quick on-and-off turns, thoroughly combine. Place dressing in heavy saucepan over medium heat. Cook until just hot. Immediately pour into hot sterilized jars. Vacuum seal as directed on page 16.

Old-fashioned Boiled Dressing

This is one of the most basic salad dressings. Its versatility is such that you can, when ready to use, add equal parts of whipping cream, sour cream, or homemade mayonnaise to change the consistency, or add fresh herbs to alter the taste. A perfect dressing for potato, cabbage, or other vegetable salads.

In top half of double boiler, beat egg yolks and all dry ingredients until thoroughly combined. Stir in vinegar and water. Place over boiling water. Cook, stirring frequently, for about 20 minutes, or until thick. Whip in vegetable oil. Immediately pour into hot sterilized jars and vacuum seal as directed on page 16.

QUANTITY:
4 ½-pint jars
PRESERVING METHOD USED:
Open kettle
STORAGE:
Vacuum-sealed—1 year
Refrigerated—2 days
May be frozen

12 egg yolks
1 teaspoon dry English mustard
1 teaspoon salt
1 heaping tablespoon superfine sugar
½ teaspoon cayenne pepper
2 cups distilled white vinegar
2 cups water
¼ cup pure vegetable oil

Jalapeño Dressing

QUANTITY:
2 ½-pint jars
PRESERVING METHOD USED:
Open kettle
STORAGE:
Vacuum-sealed—1 year
Refrigerated—2 weeks
May be frozen

2 cups fruit vinegar
3 fresh jalapeño peppers,
  seeded and minced
6 cloves garlic, peeled and
  minced
½ cup minced cilantro
¼ cup minced parsley
¼ cup minced scallions
¾ cup safflower oil
½ cup virgin olive oil

A great zesty dressing for vegetables or cold meats. It also makes an interesting addition to sandwich fillings such as tuna or egg salad.

Quickly process all ingredients together in blender. Pour into heavy saucepan over medium heat. Cook until just hot. Immediately pour into hot sterilized jars and vacuum seal as directed on page 16.

Vegetarian Dressing

Low calorie, healthful, and tasty. What more could you want? A great dressing for green or vegetable salads that can also be used on sandwiches.

Place all ingredients in heavy saucepan over medium heat. Bring to a boil. Lower heat and cook for 10 minutes. Pour into blender and puree. Again bring to a boil in heavy saucepan over medium heat. Pour into hot sterilized jars and vacuum seal as directed on page 16.

QUANTITY:
4 ½-pint jars
PRESERVING METHOD USED:
Open kettle
STORAGE:
Vacuum-sealed—1 year
Refrigerated—2 weeks
May be frozen

3 cups chopped fresh red tomatoes
3 stalks celery, cut into pieces
1 cup chopped onions
2 cloves garlic, peeled
¾ cup chopped fresh chives
¾ cup chopped fresh parsley
4 leaves fresh basil
1 tablespoon vegetarian seasoning (available in health food stores)
2 cups water
¾ cup herb vinegar

Sesame Seed Dressing

QUANTITY:
2 ½-pint jars
PRESERVING METHOD USED:
Open kettle
STORAGE:
Vacuum-sealed—1 year
Refrigerated—2 weeks
May be frozen

¾ pound fresh pot or farmer's
  cheese
2 tablespoons fresh lemon juice
1 egg yolk
½ cup Chinese sesame oil
¼ cup minced fresh coriander
¼ cup minced fresh parsley
2 cloves garlic, peeled and
  minced
½ teaspoon dried red pepper
  flakes
Dash Tabasco sauce
¼ cup heavy cream
¼ cup milk
¼ cup toasted sesame seeds

A bit of spice mellowed by the sesame oil, this dressing is used on greens, vegetables, fish, or poultry.

Quickly process all ingredients except sesame seeds in blender. Pour into heavy saucepan over medium heat. Cook until just hot. Stir in toasted sesame seeds. Pour into hot sterilized jars and vacuum seal as directed on page 16.

Fruit Salad Dressing

A perfect coating for all fruit salads, it can also be used in mixed green salads combined with citrus sections as well as on fish.

Mix all ingredients in heavy saucepan over medium heat. Cook until just hot. Immediately pour into hot sterilized jars. Vacuum seal as directed on page 16.

QUANTITY:
2 ½-pint jars
PRESERVING METHOD USED:
Open kettle
STORAGE:
Vacuum-sealed—1 year
Refrigerated—3 weeks
May be frozen

2 cups fresh raspberry puree
1 teaspoon grated fresh orange rind
1 teaspoon grated fresh lemon rind
1 teaspoon grated fresh ginger
⅛ teaspoon ground curry powder
¼ cup Triple Sec

NOTE: For serving you may wish to thin this with some yogurt, sour cream, or whipped cream.

7

Main Course Sauces

Sauces are dressings for vegetables, meats, or pasta used when you wish to add flavor and provide richness, color, and moisture. They are most generally cooked and can be made from either creams, acids, meat stocks, or chopped vegetables with added seasonings.

Cream base sauces are used for pastas, vegetables, and, occasionally, meats. Chopped vegetable and meat stock sauces are generally used on pastas and meats. Sauces having an acid base are most frequently used as cold or room temperature coverings for fish, meat, or vegetables.

Main course sauces are my favorite preserves, as they can quickly and easily provide an unexpected gourmet meal. They can all be preserved by either the open-kettle method (with rubber-edged lids and caps) or the boiling water bath as described on page 14, and may be refrigerated for short-term storage or frozen for a period of no longer than 8 months. Most will require reheating before use.

Main Course Sauces

Pesto • Gazpacho Sauce • Tuna Sauce • My Own Barbecue Sauce • Teriyaki Sauce • Creole Sauce • Fresh Tomato Sauce • Mushroom Sauce

Pesto

QUANTITY:
4 ½-pint jars
PRESERVING METHOD USED:
Freezer
STORAGE:
Vacuum-sealed—1 year
Refrigerated—2 weeks
Frozen, tightly covered—8
   months

8 cups coarsely chopped fresh
   basil, packed tightly
1½ cups fine-quality olive oil
2 cups pine nuts
2 cloves garlic, peeled and
   chopped
2 cups grated fresh Parmesan
   cheese
1 teaspoon fresh ground pepper

NOTE: Pesto can be made with
   almonds, hazelnuts, or with
   walnuts.

Pesto has become a year-round pasta or salad sauce due to the almost continuous availability of fresh basil in the supermarket. However, since basil is so prolific, it can usually be made very cheaply during the summer months. You can process in a 15-minute boiling water bath, but I really prefer the fresh taste of the frozen. This pesto is normally served on linguine or spaghetti, but it is also delicious on fish or poultry.

In bowl of food processor, using metal blade, puree all ingredients. It is best to do this in two batches. Pack into hot sterilized jars, or sterilized containers, and refrigerate or freeze as directed on page 15. To preserve, pack into hot sterilized jars, leaving ½-inch headspace. Cap and process in a 15-minute boiling water bath as directed on page 14.

Gazpacho Sauce

A perfect covering for cold beef, but it can also be used on other meats, fish, or poultry. It may be served hot or cold. You can also mix the sauce, use it immediately, or freeze it without cooking.

Place all ingredients in heavy saucepan over medium heat. Bring to a boil. Lower heat and simmer for 20 minutes, stirring frequently. Remove from heat. Immediately pour into hot sterilized jars, leaving ½-inch headspace. Cap and process in a 15-minute boiling water bath as directed on page 14.

QUANTITY:
6 ½-pint jars
PRESERVING METHOD USED:
15-minute boiling water bath
STORAGE:
Vacuum-sealed—1 year
Refrigerated—2 days
May be frozen

4 cups fresh tomato puree
2 cucumbers, peeled, seeded, and chopped fine
½ cup seeded and chopped red pepper
½ cup chopped red onions
½ cup peeled and chopped fresh celery
¼ cup peeled and grated fresh horseradish
1 tablespoon chopped fresh tarragon
2 tablespoons chopped fresh parsley
½ cup red wine vinegar
Salt and pepper to taste

Tuna Sauce

QUANTITY:
4 ½-pint containers
PRESERVING METHOD USED:
Freezer
STORAGE:
Refrigerated—no more than 12 hours
Frozen, tightly covered—6 months

12 egg yolks
¼ cup red wine vinegar
¼ cup fresh lemon juice
1½ cups virgin olive oil
1 teaspoon dry English mustard
1 teaspoon capers
6 6½-ounce cans tuna packed in olive oil, drained
½ cup drained anchovy fillets
¾ cup fresh dairy sour cream

This is one of my favorite main course sauces and is based on the sauce used in the special Italian *vitello tonnato*. I keep it in the freezer for use on cold salads, poached chicken, or veal. It can immediately turn a simple meal into a gourmet dinner.

Place egg yolks, vinegar, lemon juice, olive oil, mustard, and capers in mixing bowl of food processor. Use metal blade to puree. With machine running add tuna and anchovies. When well mixed add sour cream. Immediately pour into sterilized containers and freeze as directed on page 15.

My Own Barbecue Sauce

Like everyone, I think mine is the best. I use it on meat, fish, poultry, and, of course, ribs. I devised this sauce one summer when I was overwhelmed with tomatoes, but you can use canned tomato puree if necessary.

Place tomatoes, onions, celery, sweet peppers, and water to just barely cover in heavy saucepan over medium heat. Cook until vegetables are soft. Puree mixture in bowl of food processor, using metal blade. Place puree and all remaining ingredients in heavy saucepan over medium heat and cook, stirring frequently, for about 1 hour, or until mixture is thick. Immediately pour into hot sterilized jars, leaving ¼-inch headspace. Cap and process in a 20-minute boiling water bath as described on page 14.

QUANTITY:
4 pint jars
PRESERVING METHOD USED:
20-minute boiling water bath
STORAGE:
Vacuum-sealed—1 year
Refrigerated—2 weeks
May be frozen

10 cups peeled, cored, seeded, and chopped very ripe tomatoes
3 cups chopped onions
½ cup peeled and chopped celery
1 cup seeded and chopped sweet red pepper
1 cup light brown sugar
1 cup red wine vinegar
¼ cup fresh lemon juice
¼ cup Worcestershire sauce
1 tablespoon dried red pepper flakes
2 tablespoons dry English mustard
1 teaspoon Tabasco sauce
1 teaspoon grated fresh lemon rind
2 tablespoons commercial chili powder

Teriyaki Sauce

QUANTITY:
4 ½-pint jars
PRESERVING METHOD USED:
Open kettle
STORAGE:
Vacuum-sealed—1 year
Refrigerated—1 month
May be frozen

1 cup chopped scallions
3 cups safflower oil
1½ cups mild soy sauce
1½ cups unprocessed honey
1 tablespoon tomato paste
2 tablespoons rice vinegar
1 tablespoon grated fresh
  ginger
2 cloves garlic, peeled and
  minced
Dash Tabasco sauce

Probably not too close to the Japanese original but truly an American favorite. Great as a marinade for any meat, poultry, or fish and equally good thickened a bit with arrowroot as a gravy.

Combine all ingredients in heavy saucepan over medium heat. Bring to a boil. Lower heat and simmer for 15 minutes. Immediately pour into hot sterilized jars. Vacuum seal as directed on page 16.

Creole Sauce

Cajun (country style), Creole (New Orleans style), call it what you will. Louisiana has given us some wonderful foods. This sauce is great cooked with seafood, ground meats, and chicken. A gourmet meal done with shrimp and dirty rice.

Combine all ingredients in heavy saucepan over medium heat. Bring to a boil. Lower heat and simmer, stirring frequently, for about 1 hour. Immediately pour into hot sterilized jars, leaving ½-inch headspace. Cap and process in a 20-minute boiling water bath as directed on page 14.

QUANTITY:
4 pint jars
PRESERVING METHOD USED:
20-minute boiling water bath
STORAGE:
Vacuum-sealed—1 year
Refrigerated—1 week
May be frozen

12 cups peeled, cored, and
*   seeded very ripe tomatoes*
2 cups chopped red onions
1 cup seeded and chopped
*   sweet green peppers*
4 cloves garlic, peeled and
*   minced*
2 dried hot red peppers
1 teaspoon ground bay leaf
1 tablespoon minced fresh
*   rosemary*

Mushroom Sauce

QUANTITY:
3 pint jars
PRESERVING METHOD USED:
20-minute boiling water bath
  or freezer
STORAGE:
Vacuum-sealed—1 year
Refrigerated—1 week
Frozen—8 months

This has saved me many times, as it can change leftover meats into a superb new meal as quickly as you can open the container. You can prepare this sauce with dried French or Italian mushrooms for a more pungent taste.

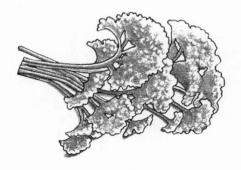

In heavy saucepan melt butter with olive oil. Add mushrooms, onions, carrots, parsley, and garlic. Sauté until mushrooms begin to lose their water and brown a bit. Remove vegetables from pan and set aside. Pour wine, water, and rosemary into mushroom pan. Bring to a boil, stirring constantly, to get any pan remains. Mix cornstarch with a small amount of red wine to dissolve it. Pour cornstarch liquid into red wine mixture. Stir until sauce is thick. Add vegetables and bring to a boil. Remove from heat and immediately pour into hot sterilized jars, leaving ½-inch headspace. Cap and process in a 20-minute boiling water bath as directed on page 14, or freeze in sterilized containers as directed on page 15.

6 *cups sliced fresh mushrooms (or same amount of soaked and sliced dried mushrooms)*
1 *cup grated onions*
½ *cup grated carrots*
¼ *cup chopped fresh parsley*
1 *clove garlic, peeled and minced*
8 *tablespoons sweet butter*
4 *tablespoons olive oil*
3 *cups good dry red wine*
1 *cup water*
1 *tablespoon chopped fresh rosemary*
¼ *cup cornstarch*
Salt and pepper to taste

Fresh Tomato Sauce

QUANTITY:
6 *pint jars*
PRESERVING METHOD USED:
*Recommended—freezer.
(However, it may be
canned in a 15-minute
boiling water bath.)*
STORAGE:
*Vacuum-sealed—1 year
Refrigerated—3 days
Frozen—8 months*

Another favorite sauce to have on hand. It can be the base for all types of Italian tomato sauces, soups, or a gravy for baked roasts and poultry. It can also be used just as is as a vegetable (drain off some of the juice) or simply cooked with lots of garlic and poured over fresh pasta. I usually keep Fresh Tomato Sauce in my freezer in pint containers.

Place all ingredients in heavy saucepan over medium heat. Bring to a boil. Lower heat and cook for 20 minutes. Pour into sterilized containers and freeze as directed on page 15. Or pour into hot sterilized jars, leaving ½-inch headspace. Cap and process in a 15-minute boiling water bath as directed on page 14.

10 cups peeled, cored, seeded, and chopped very ripe tomatoes
1 tablespoon sugar
1 teaspoon fresh ground white pepper
1 teaspoon salt (or to taste)
2 cups chopped fresh basil

8

Dessert Sauces and Syrups

Dessert or sweet sauces are, for the most part, used as toppings for ice cream, cakes, puddings, or fruit. Occasionally a sweet sauce will be used as an accompaniment to, or as a basting sauce for, meats, poultry, or game. These sauces may be made from chopped or pureed fruit or from chocolate, citrus, or liqueur bases.

Syrups may be used as toppings on breakfast breads (such as pancakes or waffles), with ice cream, as cake glazes, or in drinks. The flavor and consistency will most frequently dictate use. They are generally made from fruit puree or juice, spices, or liqueurs.

Dessert sauces and syrups can be preserved by the open-kettle method and vacuum-sealed with rubber-edged rings and caps as directed on page 16. All may be refrigerated for short-term storage or frozen for up to a period of no more than 6 months. Some will require reheating before use.

Dessert Sauces and Syrups

DESSERT SAUCES
White Chocolate Sauce • All-Purpose Pure Berry Sauce •
Cranberry Rum Sauce • Sambuca Sauce • Melba Sauce • Praline
Sauce • Shaker Lemon Sauce • Killer Chocolate Fudge Sauce
SYRUPS
Basic Sugar Syrup • Spiced Blueberry Syrup • Rum Syrup • Red
Hot Apple Syrup

White Chocolate Sauce

Unusual in its use of white chocolate, but traditional in taste. You can add variety by adding liqueur or toasted chopped nuts. A perfect topping on homemade ice cream.

Melt butter in top half of double boiler over very hot water. When melted, stir in chocolate until well blended. Add remaining ingredients. Stir to mix. Remove from heat and immediately pour into sterilized containers. Refrigerate or freeze as directed on page 15.

QUANTITY:
4 ½-pint containers
PRESERVING METHOD USED:
Refrigerator or freezer
STORAGE:
Refrigerated, tightly covered—2 weeks
Frozen, tightly covered—8 months

⅔ cup sweet butter
18 ounces white cooking chocolate
1 cup heavy cream
1 teaspoon pure vanilla extract
1 cup toasted chopped nut meats, or 2 tablespoons liqueur of your choice (optional)

All-Purpose Pure Berry Sauce

QUANTITY:
4 ½-pint containers
PRESERVING METHOD USED:
Freezer
STORAGE:
Refrigerated—3 days
Frozen, tightly covered—6
  months

This sauce can be used as is or expanded upon for dessert sauces, salads, or meats. I keep it in my freezer at all times, for use whenever a berry puree is called for.

Place berries in heavy saucepan over medium heat. Add water and lemon juice. Cover and cook until berries are soft. Remove from heat. Place berries in bowl of food processor and, using metal blade, puree. Strain puree through fine sieve to eliminate seeds. Put puree back into heavy saucepan. Taste for sweetness; add sugar if necessary (but not more than ¼ cup at a time). Bring to a boil over medium heat. Lower heat and cook for 5 minutes. Immediately pour into sterilized containers and freeze as directed on page 15.

2 quarts berries (raspberries, strawberries, blueberries, et cetera), washed and hulled
½ cup water
1 teaspoon fresh lemon juice
Sugar to taste

Cranberry Rum Sauce

QUANTITY:
4 ½-pint jars
PRESERVING METHOD USED:
Open kettle
STORAGE:
Vacuum-sealed—1 year
Refrigerated—2 weeks

2 cups sugar
1 cup water
1 cinnamon stick, broken into
  pieces
4 cups cranberries
1 cup good-quality rum
1 tablespoon cornstarch

This is wonderful served over ice cream or on baked puddings or pound cake. It can also be eaten alone with a dollop of sour cream. To serve you may add a little fresh rum and ignite each serving.

Place sugar, water, and cinnamon stick in heavy saucepan over medium heat. Bring to a boil. Lower heat and cook for 10 minutes. Remove cinnamon. Add cranberries and rum and cook for 10 more minutes. Dissolve cornstarch in a bit of rum or water. Stir into sauce. Cook for 5 minutes. Remove from heat and immediately pour into hot sterilized jars. Vacuum seal as directed on page 16.

Sambuca Sauce

A wonderful dessert topping that should be served warm. I usually make a small jar of coffee beans covered with Sambuca to be used as a garnish with this sauce.

Melt chocolate and butter in top half of double boiler over very hot water. Stir to mix. When well blended, add cocoa and coffee, stirring constantly. When well blended, add remaining ingredients and cook until sauce is thick. Pour immediately into sterilized containers and refrigerate or freeze as directed on page 15.

QUANTITY:
2 ½-pint jars
PRESERVING METHOD USED:
Freezer
STORAGE:
Refrigerated—1 month
Frozen, tightly covered—6
    months

4 ounces bittersweet chocolate
⅔ cup sweet butter
¼ cup cocoa powder
¼ cup instant espresso coffee
    powder
1 cup light brown sugar
⅓ cup half-and-half
⅓ cup Sambuca Romana

Melba Sauce

QUANTITY:
4 1/2-pint jars
PRESERVING METHOD USED:
Open kettle
STORAGE:
Vacuum-sealed—1 year
Refrigerated—1 month
May be frozen

1 cup cassis jelly (see page
   27), or fine-quality
   commercially preserved
   currant jelly
1 cup superfine sugar
3 cups fresh raspberry puree,
   strained
1 tablespoon lemon juice
1/2 teaspoon grated fresh lemon
   rind
1 teaspoon cornstarch,
   dissolved in 1 tablespoon
   cold water

Great to have on hand! Vanilla ice cream and fresh fruit topped with melba sauce is a memorable finish for any meal.

Place cassis jelly, sugar, and raspberry puree in heavy saucepan over medium heat. Bring to a boil. Add lemon juice, rind, and cornstarch dissolved in water. Cook for about 15 minutes, or until sauce is clear and thick. Immediately pour into hot sterilized jars. Vacuum seal as directed on page 16.

Praline Sauce

A very rich, extra special dessert sauce, rather like the filling for a pecan pie. Use it in moderation.

Mix egg yolks, sugar, and sweet butter together in heavy saucepan over low heat. Stir until well combined. Add cream and bourbon. Raise heat and bring to a boil. Lower heat and simmer for about 5 minutes, stirring constantly. Add pecans. Immediately pour into sterilized containers and refrigerate or freeze as directed on page 15.

QUANTITY:
4 ½-pint containers
PRESERVING METHOD USED:
Refrigerator or freezer
STORAGE:
Refrigerated—1 month
Frozen, tightly covered—8 months

8 egg yolks
1 cup light brown sugar
¼ cup sweet butter
1 cup heavy cream
3 tablespoons good bourbon
3 cups toasted pecans

Shaker Lemon Sauce

QUANTITY:
4 ½-pint jars
PRESERVING METHOD USED:
Open kettle
STORAGE:
Vacuum-sealed—1 year
Refrigerated—1 week
May be frozen

2 cups sugar
2 cups sweet butter
4 eggs
1 tablespoon grated fresh
    lemon rind
1 cup strained fresh lemon
    juice

A basic citrus sauce that has remained unchanged through generations. A refreshing sauce for all baked puddings and cakes or fruit.

Combine all ingredients in bowl of food processor, using mixing blade. When processed, scrape mixture into top half of double boiler over very hot water. Cook, stirring constantly, until sauce is thick. Add drops of boiling water if you feel sauce is too thick. Pour into hot sterilized jars and vacuum seal as directed on page 16.

Killer Chocolate Fudge Sauce

This is it. A chocoholic's dream. The ultimate chocolate dessert sauce.

Place chocolate in top half of double boiler over very hot water. Stir to melt. Add brown sugar, beaten egg yolks, and orange rind. Cook, stirring constantly, until well blended. Add heavy cream and sweet butter. Stir constantly until sauce is thick. Remove from heat. Stir in liqueur, if desired. Pour into sterilized containers and freeze as directed on page 15.

QUANTITY:
4 ½-pint jars
PRESERVING METHOD USED:
Freezer
STORAGE:
Refrigerated—1 month
Frozen, tightly covered—6 months

4 ounces unsweetened chocolate
½ cup light brown sugar
6 egg yolks
1 tablespoon grated fresh orange rind
¼ cup heavy cream
½ cup sweet butter
¼ cup liqueur of your choice (optional)

Basic Sugar Syrup

QUANTITY:
4 ½-pint jars
PRESERVING METHOD USED:
Refrigerator or freezer
STORAGE:
Refrigerated—2 weeks
Frozen, tightly covered—as
   long as you wish

2 cups sugar
4 cups cold water

After years of frustration at not having a simple syrup on hand when I was ready to poach fruit or prepare other desserts or drinks requiring it, I finally put some by. It is so easy, and a pleasure to have on hand.

Place sugar and water in heavy saucepan over medium heat. Bring to a boil. Boil for 5 minutes, stirring constantly. Remove from heat. Pour into sterilized containers and refrigerate or freeze as directed on page 15.

Spiced Blueberry Syrup

A wonderful syrup to use on breakfast breads such as pancakes or waffles. It also may be used as a dessert topping.

Put blueberries, lemon juice, orange juice, spices, and sugar in heavy saucepan over medium heat. Bring to a boil. Lower heat and cook for 20 minutes. Taste for sweetness; add sugar if necessary. Stir cornstarch dissolved in water into berry mixture. When mixture is somewhat thickened, whisk in butter a bit at a time. Remove from heat. Pour into hot sterilized jars. Vacuum seal as directed on page 16.

QUANTITY:
4 1/2-pint jars
PRESERVING METHOD USED:
Open kettle
STORAGE:
Vacuum-sealed—1 year
Refrigerated—1 month
May be frozen

4 cups fresh blueberries
1/2 cup fresh lemon juice
1/4 cup fresh orange juice
1 teaspoon ground cinnamon
1/4 teaspoon ground nutmeg
1 cup sugar
2 tablespoons cornstarch, dissolved in 1/4 cup cold water
2/3 cup sweet butter

Rum Syrup

QUANTITY:
4 ½-pint jars
PRESERVING METHOD USED:
Open kettle
STORAGE:
Vacuum-sealed—1 year
Refrigerated—3 months
May be frozen

1 cup white sugar
1 cup light brown sugar
3 cups water
1 cup dark rum
1 teaspoon grated fresh lemon
   rind
1 cup dark raisins (*optional*)
1 cup toasted chopped nuts
   (*optional*)

A multipurpose syrup for use in soaking cakes and puddings, on waffles, or in hot or cold drinks.

Place sugar and water in heavy saucepan over medium heat. Bring to a boil. Lower heat and simmer for 45 minutes, stirring frequently. Stir in rum and lemon rind, and optional ingredients, if desired. Cook for 3 minutes. Remove from heat and immediately pour into hot sterilized jars. Vacuum seal as directed on page 16.

Red Hot Apple Syrup

A spicy syrup that can be used on any dessert, pancakes, waffles, French toast, crêpes, or as flavoring in hot or cold drinks.

Place all ingredients in heavy saucepan over medium heat. Bring to a boil. Lower heat and simmer for 15 minutes. Remove from heat, cover, and let stand for 12 hours. Strain syrup. Put clear syrup in heavy saucepan over medium heat. Bring to a boil. Lower heat and cook for about 40 minutes, or until syrup is thick. Remove from heat and immediately pour into hot sterilized jars. Vacuum seal as directed on page 16.

QUANTITY:
4 ½-pint jars
PRESERVING METHOD USED:
Open kettle
STORAGE:
Vacuum-sealed—1 year
Refrigerated—1 month
May be frozen

5 cups fresh apple juice (see page 22), or fine-quality commercially canned apple juice, strained
½ cup sugar
2 cinnamon sticks, broken into pieces
¼ cup grated fresh ginger
1 hot chili pepper
1 large piece fresh orange peel

9

Miscellaneous

A little bit of everything! Some are not actually preserves but are long-lasting under refrigeration. Others are preserved to have on hand for appetizers, dips, side dishes, or accompaniments. Each has its own particular preserving or storing directions.

Miscellaneous

Sun-Dried Tomatoes (Pumate) • Marinated Mushrooms • Homemade Vinegars • Aïoli • Fresh Herbs • My Tapenade

Sun-Dried Tomatoes (Pumate)

QUANTITY:
4 ½-pint jars
PRESERVING METHOD USED:
No processing required
STORAGE:
In cool, dark place, tightly covered—6 months
May be frozen

4 cups sun-dried tomatoes
8 cloves garlic, peeled
1 teaspoon cracked black pepper
16 basil leaves
4 sprigs fresh rosemary
Excellent-quality olive oil

These can be used on pizza, in salads and sauces, as a condiment, or mixed with goat cheese and with greens as a main course. If you can't purchase sun-dried tomatoes in bulk, you can dry your own. Sprinkle coarse salt on halved plum tomatoes and either place on wire racks in very hot sun for 10 days or follow the directions of a commercial home fruit dryer.

Pack 1 cup sun-dried tomatoes in each hot sterilized jar. Mix 2 garlic cloves, ¼ teaspoon cracked black pepper, 4 basil leaves, and 1 sprig fresh rosemary in each jar. Pour in olive oil to cover. Tightly seal and store in a cool, dark place.

Marinated Mushrooms

One of my favorite cocktail tidbits. Easy to keep on hand and always delicious. I keep a half-gallon jar in my refrigerator at all times for use as an emergency appetizer, hors d'oeuvre, or salad picker-upper. When push comes to shove, marinated mushrooms can be heated and served over pasta with lots of fresh grated cheese.

Mix all ingredients together in glass bowl. Pour into half-gallon container. Tightly cover and refrigerate for at least 24 hours before using. Store under refrigeration.

QUANTITY:
1/2 gallon
PRESERVING METHOD USED:
Refrigerator
STORAGE:
*Refrigerated, tightly covered—
    at least 3 months*

*2 pounds small fresh
    mushrooms*
2 cups fine olive oil
1 cup herb vinegar
1 tablespoon grated fresh onion
8 cloves garlic, peeled
*1 teaspoon crushed dried red
    pepper flakes*
2 sprigs fresh basil
1/2 teaspoon sugar
Dash Tabasco sauce

Homemade Vinegars

QUANTITY:
1 quart
PRESERVING METHOD USED:
No processing required
STORAGE:
*In cool, dark place, tightly
    covered—3 months*

My pantry would not be complete without an array of fruit and herb vinegars. They make a world of difference in all recipes calling for any vinegar and are a special treat in salad dressings. I usually make one quart of each at a time. You can, of course, make as much as you want.

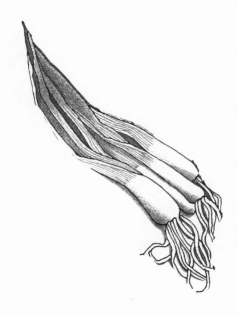

Combine vinegar with fruit or herbs. Cover tightly and store in a cool, dark place for 3 weeks. Stir or shake daily. Strain vinegar through at least 3 layers of fine cheesecloth.

For fruit vinegar: Strain into nonaluminum saucepan. Add sugar and orange peel and bring to a boil over medium heat. Cook, stirring constantly, until sugar is dissolved. Remove from heat. Discard orange peel and immediately pour into hot sterilized jars. Add a few fresh berries or pieces of fruit to each jar. Cover tightly and store in a cool, dark place.

For herb vinegar: Strain into nonaluminum saucepan and bring to a boil. Immediately pour into hot sterilized jars. Add a few pieces of garlic or shallot or 2 sprigs of fresh herb to each jar. Cover tightly and store in a cool, dark place.

FRUIT VINEGAR

4 cups fine white wine vinegar (you can also use rice wine vinegar if you like the flavor)
4 cups crushed fresh berries (cranberries, blueberries, raspberries, blackberries, gooseberries, et cetera), or chopped peaches or apples
4 tablespoons sugar
1 strip orange peel
A few whole berries or pieces of fruit for final processing

HERB VINEGAR

4 cups fine white wine vinegar or red wine vinegar
10 cloves garlic, peeled and crushed, or 1 cup peeled minced shallots, or 1 cup minced fresh tarragon, rosemary, sage, thyme, basil, or chives
Whole pieces of garlic or shallot, or 2 sprigs of each fresh herb

Aïoli

QUANTITY:
2 ½-pint jars
PRESERVING METHOD USED:
Freezer
STORAGE:
Refrigerated—1 day
Frozen, tightly covered—up to
3 months

8 *large cloves garlic, peeled*
and chopped
2 *egg yolks*
¼ *teaspoon salt*
2 *teaspoons fresh lemon juice*
or herb vinegar
2 *cups extra fine olive oil*

Aïoli is generally used in Mediterranean cooking, but it is a versatile preserve and can touch up many types of food. It is essentially a rich garlic mayonnaise. It is traditionally served with poached fish in a dish called *bourride*. I use it in meat or fish salads, as a main course sauce, or as a vegetarian's delight covering a steamed vegetable platter.

Place garlic, egg yolks, salt, and lemon juice or vinegar in blender. Process at medium speed to mix thoroughly. Through hole in lid slowly add olive oil, drop by drop. Keep adding and processing until all oil is absorbed and sauce is thick. Do not overbeat, as sauce will get too thick. Scrape out of jar and pour into sterilized containers. Refrigerate or freeze as directed on page 15. If you freeze the sauce, you will have to thaw and quickly process it before using.

My Tapenade

A wonderful sauce/condiment/relish to be used on pasta, baked potatoes, steamed vegetables, or grilled fish. A perfect lunch—tossed green salad and a huge baked potato popped open and topped with tapenade and sour cream. When used with pasta add lots of grated fresh Parmesan cheese.

Heat ¾ cup olive oil in heavy saucepan over medium heat. Add onion and garlic. Cook, stirring constantly, for 5 minutes. Add peppers. Lower heat and cook for about 10 minutes, or until peppers are wilted. Stir in all remaining ingredients except 4 tablespoons olive oil. Raise heat to high and cook for 5 minutes, or until almost all liquid is absorbed. Immediately pour into hot sterilized jars. Cover each with 1 tablespoon olive oil. Vacuum seal as directed on page 16.

QUANTITY:
4 ½-pint jars
PRESERVING METHOD USED:
Open kettle
STORAGE:
Vacuum-sealed—1 year
Refrigerated—3 weeks
May be frozen

¾ cup extra fine olive oil
¼ cup finely chopped onions
3 garlic cloves, peeled and minced
1 cup seeded and chopped sweet green peppers
1 cup seeded and chopped sweet red peppers
½ cup seeded and chopped sweet yellow peppers
1½ cups roasted walnuts, finely chopped
2 cups minced imported black olives
⅓ cup herb vinegar
⅓ cup minced fresh parsley
Salt and pepper to taste
4 tablespoons extra fine olive oil

Fresh Herbs

QUANTITY:
1 cup
PRESERVING METHOD USED:
No processing required
STORAGE:
Bottled—6 months
Refrigerated—1 week
Frozen, tightly sealed—1 year

These are an absolute necessity. If you grow your own, be sure to put some by for the winter months. It does make a difference in any recipe calling for herbs. There are two easy methods to preserve fresh herbs.

FREEZER METHOD
Place herbs and oil in blender. Process until mixture is a thick puree. Measure out table-spoons (or use physician's small disposable paper pill dispens-ers). Wrap in aluminum foil and seal. Freeze. When frozen put foil-wrapped tablespoons in plastic bags and label with amount and type. This just makes it easier to use small amounts at a time.

BOTTLE METHOD
Pack as many clean fresh herbs of one kind as you can into a ½-pint sterilized jar. Cover with extra fine olive oil. Tightly seal and store in a cool, dark place. When ready to use, take out the amount of herb you need and use as you would fresh. You can rinse the oil off if you wish. You can also use the olive oil in salads and sauces.

FREEZER METHOD
2 cups packed fresh herbs (basil, parsley, rosemary, et cetera)
¼ cup extra fine olive oil

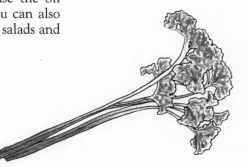

Miscellaneous

Index

165

172

About the Author

Judith Choate is a freelance writer whose books and articles range from cookbooks to children's books. She ran her own catering business until 1985, and is the co-author of *The Gift Giver's Cookbook* and *Patchwork for Kids*, among others. Judith Choate lives in New York City.